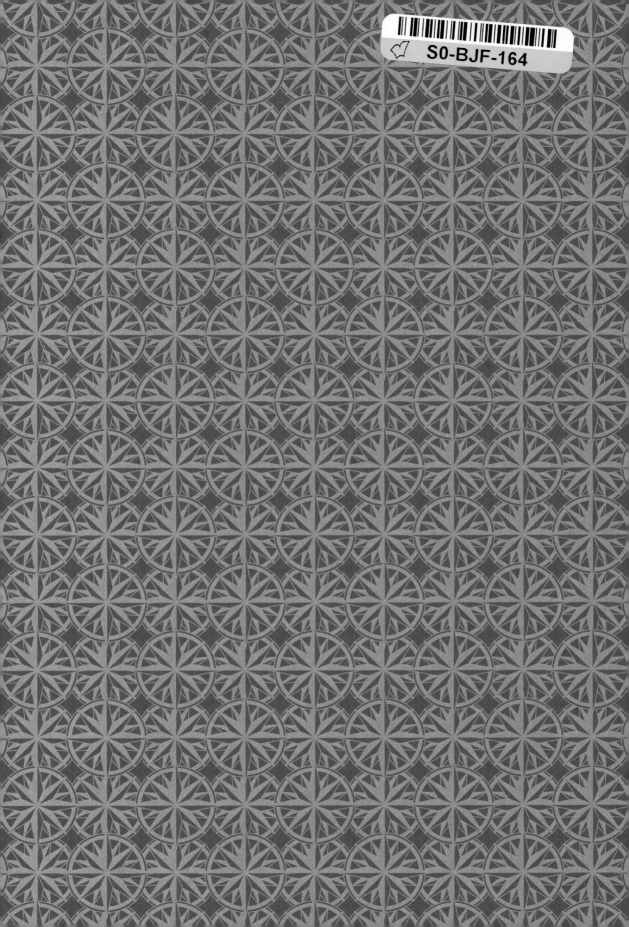

PATHWAYS
TO DISCOVERY

Exploring America's National Trails

A BOY SCOUT STARTS A CAMPFIRE NEAR KENTUCKY'S SHELTOWEE TRACE.

PATHWAYS
TO DISCOVERY

Exploring America's National Trails

Prepared by the Special Publications Division
National Geographic Society, Washington, D.C.

PATHWAYS TO DISCOVERY:
Exploring America's National Trails

Contributing Authors: Leslie Allen,
Thomas B. Allen, Ron Fisher, Jane R. McCauley,
Cynthia Russ Ramsay, Scott Thybony

Contributing Photographers: Tom Bean,
Annie Griffiths Belt, Rich Frishman,
Raymond Gehman, Scott Goldsmith, David Hiser,
Robb Kendrick, Joel Sartore, Pete Souza,
Medford Taylor, Ana M. Venegas

Published by
The National Geographic Society
Gilbert M. Grosvenor,
    President and Chairman of the Board
Owen R. Anderson,
    Executive Vice President
Robert L. Breeden, *Senior Vice President,*
    Publications and Educational Media
William R. Gray, *Director, Book Division*

Prepared by
The Special Publications Division
Donald J. Crump, *Director*
Bonnie S. Lawrence, *Assistant Director*

Staff for this book
Mary Ann Harrell, *Managing Editor*
Dennis R. Dimick, *Illustrations Editor*
Jody Bolt, *Art Director*
Rebecca Lescaze, *Senior Researcher*
Victoria Cooper, *Researcher*
Margery G. Dunn, *Consulting Editor*
Leslie Allen, Richard M. Crum, Toni Eugene,
    Jane R. McCauley, H. Robert Morrison,
    Picture Legend Writers
Jody Bolt, Joseph F. Ochlak,
    Map Research and Production
Sandra F. Lotterman, *Editorial Assistant*
Artemis S. Lampathakis, *Illustrations Assistant*

Engraving, Printing, and Product Manufacture
George V. White, *Director,* and
Vincent P. Ryan, *Manager,*
    Manufacturing and Quality Management
David V. Showers, *Production Manager*
Lewis R. Bassford, *Production Project Manager*
Timothy H. Ewing, *Assistant Production Manager*

Rosamund Garner, Lisa A. LaFuria,
    Katharine N. Old, Dru M. Stancampiano,
    Marilyn J. Williams, *Staff Assistants*

Anne K. McCain, *Indexer*

NEAR THE ROUTE PROPOSED FOR THE BENTON MACKAYE TRAIL

PRECEDING PAGES:
BEARGRASS COVERS A MEADOW
ON THE WESTERN SLOPES
OF MOUNT HOOD,
A LANDMARK OF
THE PACIFIC CREST TRAIL.

IN NORTH CAROLINA'S GREAT SMOKY MOUNTAINS, WILD IMPATIENS THRIVES BESIDE A RIVULET.

Contents

HIKERS FIND SHADE AT UTAH'S SLIDE ROCK ARCH ON THE PARIA CANYON TRAIL.

Getting away from it all, hikers in Golden Gate National Recreation Area survey the San Francisco skyline from a steep slope in the Marin headlands. In 1968 Congress established the National Trails System; it classifies trails as scenic, historic, or recreational. Often set in urban areas, recreation trails offer an escape and a change of pace; they may be in federal and state parks, in national forests, or on private lands. Pathways to Discovery samples national trails in five U.S. regions.

PROLOGUE

By Ron Fisher

*I*think I first realized that it was possible to walk for pleasure—as opposed to walking simply to get somewhere—when I was a boy. The Rock Island Railroad ran through West Chester, the Iowa village where I grew up, and my friends and I explored along its tracks. We hunted rabbits in winter and shady spots in summer. We put our ears against the rails and tried to hear trains coming, and in those days one or two did every day.

According to family lore, in December of 1918, when my great-grandfather David Fisher died of a heart attack while working on his farm, a blizzard had closed the county roads. The train made a special stop to pick up his body and the mourners to carry them into town for the funeral. My memories are brighter. I remember learning to recognize orioles and chickadees along the tracks, and I can still feel the crunch of cinders underfoot. A spectacular expanse of brilliant pink shooting stars triggered my sister Kathy's life-long interest in prairie wildflowers.

Mostly I recall from my childhood walks the satisfaction of starting off to look for something interesting and of sometimes finding it: a dead snake, an unusual bottle thrown from a train, some nameless plant in bloom.

Such simple pleasures are still the primary attraction of walking and the fundamental appeal of trails. And today Americans are hitting the trail for pleasure as never before. Hikers are hiking, bikers biking, riders riding, joggers jogging, and skiers skiing all across the land. In the National Trails System alone, established by Congress in 1968, there are now eight national scenic trails, nine national historic trails, and more than 780 national recreation trails. All together they offer about 35,000 miles of recreational opportunities. Though many are unfinished, slow but steady progress is being made.

The National Trails System Act recognized two major scenic trails—the Appalachian and the Pacific Crest—and authorized the study of additional routes for eventual management by the National Park Service or other agencies. The U.S. Forest Service, the Fish and Wildlife Service, and the Bureau of Land Management all administer trails under their own jurisdiction.

The national scenic trails, which must be at least 100 miles long and suitable for walking, are the Potomac Heritage, the Appalachian, the Florida, the Natchez Trace, the Ice Age (entirely within Wisconsin), the North Country, the Continental Divide, and the Pacific Crest.

National historic trails include some marked highways on or near the original routes. The present nine are the Iditarod in Alaska, the Overmountain Victory in the southern Appalachians, the Trail of Tears, the Santa Fe, the Oregon, the Mormon Pioneer, the Nez Perce, the Juan Bautista de Anza, and the Lewis and Clark, longest of all at 3,700 miles.

National recreation trails include many shorter trails, often in urban or suburban settings, which may be open to some motorized use. They can be found in federal or state parks and forests, local parks and preserves, or on private land, or combinations of any type. San Francisco, for example, looks forward to the completion of 800 miles of greenway in two sprawling loops, a bayside and a ridge-crest route; this system will include the 31-mile East Bay Skyline National Recreation Trail and designated paths in Golden Gate National Recreation Area. These links will thread their way carefully through a highly urbanized but extremely beautiful area.

Although some of our trails are new, many have been in use for centuries. Indians, seeking the easiest ways through the forests and mountains of the East, often followed animal trails. Their footpaths, in turn, became the horse trails and wagon roads of the early European settlers and in time highways replaced those. The Pennsylvania Turnpike was once a muddy track barely wider than a bison.

Today many trails face serious problems that worry their proponents. Funding looms large in their list of concerns. To acquire the land (or easements) for a trail, to clear it and blaze it and map it and publish its data—all this is expensive. In times of government deficits and cutbacks, much of the cost must be met by private donations. And without volunteer labor, most of today's trails would not exist. Clearing is just a beginning. A steep trail can soon become a gully, or a flat trail can become a thicket, without maintenance. Labor means grueling physical exertion, so strenuous that one Florida volunteer remarked, "If they paid me for this, I probably wouldn't do it."

Moreover, there may be resistance to trail development from landowners. A few of them still speak of "riffraff" or "damned hippies" or "damned yuppies" and worry about litter, vandalism, and loss of privacy. Almost always, however, such fears prove groundless. Conflicts between users of a trail are less frequent but do occur, such as wrangles between mountain bikers and horseback riders. Hikers complain when a trail becomes so popular that crowds destroy its appeal. On occasion, the fortunes of a trail may be affected by disagreements in the tangled underbrush of bureaucracy, when paperwork moves at the pace of a tired hiker with blisters.

In *Pathways to Discovery* you'll find a sampler of trails. Not all of them are end-to-end parts of the National Trails System, but all cross federal land to some extent and all will lead to the discovery of something unexpected. Some major trails, which the National Geographic Society has covered recently or extensively, are not here, but some new ones are. Five regional chapters—focused on the Southeast, the Northeast, the Midwest, the Rocky Mountains, and the Far West—present three trails each.

Among them are the Benton MacKaye Trail, begun in Georgia, which honors the father of the Appalachian Trail. When completed, it will meander for 250 remote miles through the deciduous forests of the southern Appalachians. In the Northeast, Vermont's Long Trail and the trails in the White Mountains of New Hampshire offer very different highland hiking. The North Country Trail, 3,200 miles long, runs from upstate New York into North Dakota; you'll find Michigan's lonely lakeshore segment a vivid contrast to riverside woodland and farms and sociable little towns in southern Ohio. In the Rockies, you'll try thin-air cross-country skiing on the 10th Mountain Trail in Colorado, desert backpacking in red-rock Paria Canyon on the Utah-Arizona border. The Far West has its own striking distinctions. You'll climb restive slopes of the high Cascades in Oregon, on the 2,600-mile Pacific Crest Trail. This route runs from Canada to Mexico through rugged terrain in the coastal states; and it contrasts vividly with Santa Barbara's Front Country trails, within walking distance of city streets.

Throughout the book you'll find common threads: a preoccupation with weather and trail surface; a curiosity about plants and animals; an ear cocked for historical nuggets; and frequent and pleasurable rests.

The diversity of the trails explored here matches the diversity of the country. There's a terrain for every taste.

But enough of prologue. Let's hit the trail.

Mount
St. Helens
Trails

WASHINGTON

Pacific Crest
Trail

OREGON

IDAHO

MONTANA

WYOMING

Continental Divide Trail

North
Country Trail

NORTH DAKOTA

SOUTH DAKOTA

NEBRASKA

NEVADA

East Bay
Skyline Trail

Pacific Crest Trail

CALIFORNIA

Santa Barbara
Trails

UTAH

10th Mountain
Trail

Colorado
Trail

COLORADO

KANSAS

Paria Canyon
Trail

ARIZONA

NEW MEXICO

OKLAHOMA

TEXAS

*N*ational network of trails encompasses California canyons, Rocky Mountain
ramparts, Florida pinewoods, and windswept Vermont crags. As diverse in type as in
terrain, these pathways range from the long-established Pacific Crest National
Scenic Trail to the still incomplete Florida National Scenic Trail. Of more than 800 routes
in the system, 15 figure prominently in this book; dots indicate unfinished portions.
Nine historic trails, not mapped here, often lie near highways.

MINNESOTA

MICHIGAN

WISCONSIN

Ice Age Trail

Cedar Valley Nature Trail

IOWA

Kewash Nature Trail

ILLINOIS

INDIANA

MICHIGAN

North Country Trail

OHIO

MISSOURI

Sheltowee Trace

KENTUCKY

TENNESSEE

Dripstone Trail

Benton MacKaye Trail

ARKANSAS

Natchez Trace

ALABAMA

MISSISSIPPI

LOUISIANA

MAINE

VERMONT

NEW YORK

White Mountains Trails

NEW HAMPSHIRE

Long Trail

MASSACHUSETTS

Southern New England Trunkline Trail

RHODE ISLAND

North Country Trail

CONNECTICUT

PENNSYLVANIA

NEW JERSEY

Potomac Heritage Trail

DELAWARE

MARYLAND

WEST VIRGINIA

Appalachian Trail

Washington & Old Dominion Railroad Regional Park

VIRGINIA

NORTH CAROLINA

SOUTH CAROLINA

GEORGIA

FLORIDA

Florida Trail

—————— trails or portions featured in this book

—————— other trails or portions mentioned

0   500 Miles

0   500 Kilometers

*D*ashing *through the snow and ice in the 1989 Iditarod Trail Sled Dog Race, Joe Garnie mushes toward Nome; fleecy booties protect his huskies' feet. At 3,500-foot Rainy Pass, highest point on the trail, teams cross the Alaska Range (opposite). The 1,150-mile race from Anchorage takes its name from the Iditarod Trail, once a vital winter link with the goldfields of interior Alaska. In 1925 mushers carrying serum raced along the route to end a diphtheria epidemic in Nome; Congress designated the Iditarod a historic trail in 1978.*

FOLLOWING PAGES: Ruts recall the wagons of a 19th-century settler as tourists pass by Seal Rock on their way to the tree-lined bank of the North Platte River, route of the Oregon Trail in Nebraska. The 2,100-mile-long pathway led thousands of pioneers from Missouri to the Pacific coast; in 1978 Congress authorized it as a national historic trail.

*U*nexpected element of the national system, the Dripstone Trail winds through
Blanchard Springs Caverns in Arkansas. Guided by U.S. Forest Service staff, visitors on
the 0.4-mile recreation trail admire stalactites in the Soda Straw Room.

*K*entucky's Natural Bridge—65 feet high, 20 feet wide, spanning 78 feet—
affords vistas of the Red River Gorge area. Wind and water created the sandstone
structure, one among scores of natural arches within a 30-square-mile
region at the northern end of the Sheltowee Trace.
From the Sheltowee's 257 rugged miles to the cypress swamps of the Florida Trail,
hiking routes of the Southeast offer notable diversity.

THE
SOUTHEAST

By Jane R. McCauley

The Sheltowee Trace

KENTUCKY

TENNESSEE

*L*egend holds it was a local character known as Devil Sal, hefty and mean, who gave the Pinch-Em-Tight Trail in Kentucky's Red River Gorge its name. Besides her fondness for moonshine, she liked the huckleberries that thrived on the high ridges. Returning from picking berries one day with her two sons, she became wedged in a narrow crevice. The younguns fled, leaving Devil Sal stuck with her buckets on her shoulders. It was a couple of days before she lost enough weight to free herself.

That legend piqued my curiosity. So, on a glorious Indian summer day in October, I set out along the trail. "An easy stroll on a warm spring or autumn day," advises the guidebook *Kentucky's Land of the Arches*. Pumpkin hues, golds, and reds flecked the oaks and black gums. Layers of dry pine needles crackled underfoot. Splashes of sunlight danced across an occasional tree root. A ridge narrowed until the path hugged the edge of a cliff. I was overwhelmed by the stillness. I noticed tiny sounds—the chirps of hidden birds, the whisper of a breeze, the rasping of my vest zipper as the breeze blew cool or the sun struck warm. Did I hear footsteps? Dense woods can do that to a hiker.

Through the trees to my right I looked out across the gorge, far too big to capture in a single glance. More than 60 million years of weathering created this 30-square-mile geological wonderland of the Cumberland Plateau, reminding me of a wooded Grand Canyon in miniature. Within it, thousands of rock shelters vary in length from a few feet to a hundred yards. Immense pinnacles and spires jut into emptiness, and scores of stone arches rise on ridgetops and in valleys. Above it all, buzzards circle like specks in endless sky.

Such was the beginning of my explorations along Kentucky's Sheltowee Trace. Established in 1979 as a national recreation trail, it begins in the northeast, near Morehead and about 30 miles south of the Ohio River, links up with the trails threading the Red River Gorge, then zigzags southward through the state before ending in Tennessee. Most of its 257 miles cross the Daniel Boone National Forest, a 670,000-acre reserve honoring the famous woodsman. Sheltowee, meaning Big Turtle, is the name given Boone by the Shawnee who captured and adopted him. To Boone, said his first biographer, these wooded lands were "a series of wonders, and a fund of delight."

Verne Orndorff is one person who has long shared Boone's sentiments. In 1979 he mapped the trace while working as a landscape architect for the U.S. Forest Service. Now retired, he maintains his interest in it. On a rainy

*H*idden by a hiker's hat, "Recreation" completes an official marker near midpoint of the Sheltowee. Designated in 1979, the trace attracts many out-of-state visitors. Easy access from local roads makes it a popular choice for day hikers.

afternoon, too wet for the trail, we chatted at his home in Winchester. "People kept asking if there was a path through the Daniel Boone National Forest. And, of course, there wasn't." Verne explained that the trace was designed as a way to scenic wonders like the Red River Gorge. "It was also created," he added, "as a route to historical sites." Among those he mentioned were the Warriors' Path, an Indian route; the Boone Trace, route of pioneer settlers; and the 19th-century iron furnaces scattered through the area.

We talked about some of the difficulties in developing the Sheltowee. Acquiring easements across private property, he said, was often complicated by confusing records in county courthouses. "To bypass the rocky cliffs we have around here," he went on, "trails sometimes ended up on less than favorable grades. Then, clear-cutting has left sprouts, and their regrowth is difficult to keep up with." The planners tried to meet the needs of as many groups as they could, he said, allowing horses and off-road vehicles in some stretches.

To Verne, the Sheltowee's greatest asset is probably the diversity it gives hikers. Cliffs, coves, and ridges in the northern stretches provide rigorous terrain. Farther south, flatter lands crossed by numerous streams offer different challenges. Then, too, you can bed down under the stars in the backcountry, or find accommodations in the lodges and cabins at state parks. Usually stops for food, mail, and supplies are no more than three days' walk apart. And stretches can be hiked without a backpack.

*R*oaming the trace, I soon took on a routine. Each evening I would take out the Forest Service maps and highlight a route for the next day. I ascended crests, followed ridgelines, crossed lonely gravel roads, forded a few chilly little streams. I watched for the white diamond blazes (the emblem of trails on Forest Service land) or the turtle logo trail markers. Little country stores supplied yogurt and fruit for picnic lunches.

Wherever I went I found beauty. Morning fogs floated over blustery ridges, breaking into wispy streamers. At times, gray skies broke to let sunlight crimson the hillsides where aging little tobacco barns cure tiers of yellowing leaf. Gusty winds added mystery to dark, mossy recesses. Steep slopes subsided into rhododendron thickets concealing waterfalls that flowed musically. In meadows beside country roads, clumps of tawny beard grass bowed and bobbed like puppets.

Weekends brought out the crowds in the parks, five ranger districts, and recreation areas along the Sheltowee. Parking lots were jammed. One Saturday, photographer Annie Griffiths Belt and I stopped by the Turkey Foot Recreation Area near McKee. Boy Scouts of Troop 118 from Richmond were practicing tying knots, learning to lay a fire, and joking around. Not far from them we met visitors from Ohio who had been turned away from campgrounds near the gorge. They complained of increasing damage from trail bikes on the Sheltowee, and only a few minutes later four bikers came whirring up. Radios were blaring country music from nearby picnic tables.

On weekdays, however, I never saw more than four people all told. In the quiet I would hum country music or Stephen Foster's songs to myself. After all, Daniel Boone's voice occasionally rang through these same forests. Sometimes I would rest beside a tree and try to imagine the bear hunter with his long rifle at hand. Then again. . . . I never ran into a bear.

The rich heritage of Daniel Boone came back to me the day Annie and I stumbled onto Bush's country store at Zachariah, a hamlet on Route 11. For years it has served hikers from Natural Bridge State Park. Earnest Bush, who owns it, traces his ancestry to the original Boonesborough settlers.

Stained by age, the floor creaked as we entered. Alvina Bush, in coral slacks and blue sweater, smiled from behind the massive old brass cash register. A hodgepodge of goods filled shelves and bins: jeans, shoes, hunting gear; cans of beans, applesauce, and fruits. I bought an apple, Annie a candy bar, and we settled down beside the potbellied stove, which was going strong. Earnest sat close by, whittling one cedar stick after another. "Sharp knife, weak mind," he assured us. "That's all it takes to whittle." He had more than a hundred of his deftly carved canes in the back room. "Why do you like whittling?" I asked. "Oh, it keeps my mind and hands busy." Without lifting his head he asked, "Where y'all from?" "Washington, D.C." "Oh, up there."

Dismissing the Capital, Earnest talked about his six grandchildren and their frequent visits. Folks came and went as we talked, but he told us that the new highway was taking traffic away from the store. As we started to leave, he said, "Now you be sure and come back."

A visit to the Bushs' store has become something of a local tradition. Wherever I went, people spoke of it. Other customs, too, contribute to the Sheltowee's distinctive character. The area is a center of old-time and bluegrass music. Local festivals in fall, spring, and summer ring with the sounds of dulcimers, banjos, and guitars. Churches hold gospel sings and revivals. And a hungry hiker is always welcome at Wednesday-night church suppers.

Then there're the traditional crafts. In McCreary County, on the Tennessee line, are specialists in one of the most appealing—making cornhusk dolls. Annie and I were lucky to meet a native of the region who agreed to introduce us to some of these craftspeople if we promised to respect their privacy. I'll simply say they live a few "Appalachian miles" from the trace.

One, who likes to be called Georgie, left a mill job more than a decade ago to specialize in angels. We sat on her porch and watched her begin by shaping a white head around a wad of cotton, then making arms out of wire.

Early one morning we reached Pat's home, a frame house literally wedged into a hillside. She was preparing for a show in North Carolina. Cornshucks were boiling in a pot of bright pink dye on the electric stove; others, a rosy tint, dried beside the sink. Fresh coffee was brewing, and a shy cat huddled beneath a chair. At a table in the living room, Pat was completing a doll. Boxes of wreaths, dolls, and flowers cluttered the space around her. "Cornshucking has enabled me to travel and to put biscuits on the table," she said. With painstaking care, she ties husks with string, then applies glue to the silk for hair. Curls are formed around a pencil. Curling irons shape skirts. A face drawn in India ink gives each doll its own character. "One," Pat recalled, "was rejected by the marketing association because it looked like it was choking." Accessories include umbrellas, hats, and egg baskets. She has devised her own technique for making life-size roses, which she has taught to her 80-year-old mother and her teenage daughter.

By teaching her daughter, Pat is assuring that a traditional craft will endure through another generation. In much the same way, setting aside the Sheltowee Trace has promised that a landscape rich in history will be there for others to savor as I did. Although the gorge holds a limestone arch called Moonshiner's, I never met anybody as ornery as Devil Sal.

The Florida Trail

FLORIDA

J im Kern had a vision: to create a continuous footpath through the state of
Florida. One day, he thought, it could even be linked to the Appalachian
Trail and then a hiker could go the length of the eastern states, beginning in
the far south in winter. So in 1966 Kern set out northward in the most difficult
terrain possible, from the Tamiami Trail through the heart of Big Cypress
Swamp. A real estate agent by profession, he was also a nature photographer
and writer, and an inexperienced hiker although he had sampled the Appalachian Trail. He carried only basic supplies, including a machete, map, and
compass. His 45-pound pack was heavier than he liked, but he would manage.

For 160 sweaty miles Kern slashed and cut and plodded his way through
shoulder-high grasses, cabbage-palm hammocks, and cattle country. Occasionally, pack and all, he had to wade through waist-deep water—in snake
and gator habitat—and more than once he got lost. But he pushed on, ending
his journey in 12 days at Highlands Hammock State Park in central Florida.

Within months he had attracted enough supporters to establish the Florida Trail Association, or FTA. (Like him, many had come from the Northeast.)
The FTA would determine the route of the country's only subtropical trail, kin-
dle enthusiasm for it, fight for it, and assume responsibility for building and
maintaining it. Today the association has a membership of 5,000. More than
1,000 miles have been blazed. A thousand miles to thaw in, from a northern
perspective; "a couch potato's worst nightmare," one visitor remarked. In 1983
the trail was added to the national scenic list.

Backpacking those thousand miles today, or day hiking a shorter bit,
opens primeval scenery suggesting the Florida known to the Indians. It's
amazingly diverse. In subtropical southern Florida, a 12-inch change in elevation can mean a dramatic change of setting, for local plants are exquisitely
adapted to variations of drainage. Cypress flourishes in the lowest, wettest
spots; grass on slightly higher ground; pine on drier soil; hardwoods in the
hammocks, or so-called tree islands.

While naturalists revel in the distinctive creatures of each community,
any observant visitor finds a showcase of wonders. Alligators lurk in dark
pools; snowy egrets and glossy ibis feed on the fringes of marshes; deer graze
in glades. Intricate orchids and spikelike bromeliads cling to swamp trees; saw
palmettos spread their fanlike leaves to carpet the pinewoods; cabbage palms
dot the prairie. And for those who listen, the land speaks of its special qualities: the clacking of palm fronds, like living castanets; the booming nine-beat
call of the barred owl; the faint sifting of sand, the lapping of waves.

So it struck me as I went exploring. I began in February, in the south. This
is an ideal time, with rain (relatively) scant and insects (relatively) few and temperatures (relatively) cool. I could capture the changing of the seasons, from
early flowering in the swamps to greening of the forests farther north.

Like any other trail, this one has its distinctive challenges: year-round humidity in the swamps, slippery ravines and cable bridges to negotiate. Though vegetation can be thick enough to limit the view, pathways are usually clear. National forest and state park or forest personnel, assisted by Boy Scouts and members of other youth groups, help maintain them. But the bulk of the task falls to dedicated FTA volunteers.

Almost every weekend, except in the hottest months, parties go out armed with mowers and machetes, picks and shovels, posthole-diggers and block-and-tackle gear. "We have one of the best volunteer organizations in the country," says Mason Miller of the U.S. Forest Service. It took less than a day with the Wednesday Wonders, veteran trail builders from the Tampa area, to convince me he's right. They're members of the Suncoast chapter, largest of 12. Besides trail work, they sponsor biking, birding, canoeing, and camping.

We reached the Little Manatee River State Recreation Area, 25 miles southeast of Tampa, about 9 a.m. Section leader Fred Mulholland, in fatigues, was giving out assignments with the precision of a drill sergeant. "I'm experienced at this," he confided. "Been doing it for twenty years." The Wonders, he explained, were adding 19 bridges on this popular new loop—one of the FTA's "isolated" routes, not linked to the primary trail.

Leaving the pickups in a field, we trekked down a narrow path until we were engulfed in scrub oaks and palmettos. Here and there, yellow jessamine and branches of fringe tree were vivid in stray beams of sunshine. We came to a streambed with clumps of moss, decaying leaves, and ferns lining its gentle slopes. In this peaceful setting, the work went briskly. Twenty-four-foot beams were dragged into place with block and tackle, then bolted onto sleepers. Fred patrolled the scene, offering advice when asked. No one stopped except to wipe away sweat or soothe an aching muscle. Yet the mood was lighthearted. "Those over 95 paint blazes," chuckled sun-browned veteran John Bell. By midafternoon one bridge was finished and logs were in place for another. Fresh white blazes gleamed from tree trunks along 6.5 miles of trail.

This group of 15 ranged in age from the early 30s to the 80s. The Suncoast chapter alone has devoted 8,500 hours of work in one year. Without such volunteers the trail would not exist. But the help of private landowners, local authorities, and state and federal agencies is needed if Kern's dream is to be fulfilled. Lengthy stretches are mapped but missing in the south, between the Big Cypress National Preserve and Lake Okeechobee; in central Florida; and in the Panhandle. These must be secured quickly, Mason Miller cautioned me, before private lands pass into the hands of developers. Often individual landowners refuse access to hikers because they fear vandalism or liability in case of accidents, and 15 percent of this system is on private land. (Only 15 miles, happily, run through an Air Force bombing range, where hikers need USAF permission to enter.) Especially important state agencies include the Department of Natural Resources and the regional water management districts.

One recent agreement involves the South Florida WMD and the FTA in Palm Beach and Martin Counties. It allows access to the 21,935-acre John G. and Susan H. DuPuis, Jr., Reserve, once the weekend retreat of a Miami family. This is a useful addition in a blank swatch east of Lake Okeechobee. "We'll construct the trailhead and provide equipment if they'll develop the trails," Fred Schiller told me. He's a recreational planner for the district, and we were jouncing across the area in his truck, with FTA members Mary Jones and Jerry Underwood. Potholes made driving—and walking—exasperating; they're the work of feral hogs, and we saw more than one family of razorbacks at water holes. Fred suggested that hunting could control the overpopulation of pigs. Trails, he hastened to add, would be closed to hikers on days when the reserve was opened for hunting. Here and elsewhere on public land, hikers don't need to carry FTA identification, which they must do on private holdings. (Members accept responsibility for their own safety.)

By midday we had sampled ponds and marshes, wet prairies and cypress forests suited to the novice or the seasoned backpacker. Those seeking a smoother trail, however, might prefer Jonathan Dickinson State Park, west of Jupiter Island on the Atlantic coast. Its vistas aren't as broad, but it's a wonderful place to study nature close up. Incidentally, it also has trails designated for horseback riding. Florida's trail partisans include members of the Affiliated Horse Organizations of Florida, AHOOF for short.

This 11,300-acre park commemorates a Quaker merchant from Pennsylvania. Sailing home from Jamaica with his wife and infant son and a number of slaves, he was shipwrecked on Jupiter Island. While a captive of local Indians, he kept a diary that was published in 1699 after his party escaped. I welcomed an outing here with Mary Jones, who helped map and blaze the trail and knows the country Dickinson saw. We had a perfect afternoon: The mercury hadn't climbed past 70 and there was no sign of a shower. Almost at once we nearly collided with an armadillo, hunched in the middle of the path. Startled, it jumped straight into the air, then scurried into the underbrush in a whirl of fine sand. The sand gave a gentle whissh underfoot, and pinecones crunched. "We're actually walking on ancient sand dunes left as the ocean receded," Mary remarked; she explained that the stands of trees are south Florida's variant of sand pine. She was constantly alerting me to a wayward frond of saw palmetto; the sharp teeth along the leafstalk leave a painful memory. The Indians relished their black berries, but Dickinson compared the flavor to "rotten Cheese steep'd in *Tobacco*."

Mary identified plants harder to spot. She pointed to rosemary (not the cooking herb), its leaves curled as tight as needles to conserve water. We paused to admire the shimmery iridescent blue of a scrub lizard. A pawpaw flower reminded me of a little brown puppy's face turned to look at us. We caught glimpses of scrub jays in their blue collars. Mary broke off a sprig of wax myrtle, or southern bayberry. Some believe, she said, that a bit of it in your hat will ward off mosquitoes. Perhaps it was working.

Not so on the afternoon I spent in Collier-Seminole State Park, southeast of Naples. I could have used garlands of wax myrtle even though it wasn't peak mosquito season. The nature trail, says the FTA guidebook, may be "the only true tropical trail" on the U.S. mainland. Here cypress swamp meets tropical forest. Ah, romance. Insects abound, the western part of the trail is nearly always wet, and often the paths are overgrown. Though wildlife is abundant, it has dense greenery to hide in. I did see a gopher locked in its mottled shell—gopher, in Florida, usually means a tortoise. I saw deer tracks, and the wide grooves of an alligator's tail in a water hole dried by drought. Campers are warned to hang food out of the reach of black bears. How could bears in their heavy pelts survive this heat? Nobody ever explained this to my satisfaction.

The distinctive and enticing feature of this park is its vegetation, which evokes the West Indies. Strangler figs weave upward and into the canopy.

Masses of brown limbs, laden with grayish lichens, intersect. Conspicuous in these tangles are the wild royal palms. Their smooth gray trunks soar to sixty feet or more; their deep green leaves grow as long as twelve feet. Certainly they're impressive. Yet I agree with John Muir, who maintained palms are not graceful plants. Though I like the rattle of palm fronds, I prefer the shaggy look of cypresses. And these are prettiest, I think, when they begin to unfurl their buds, cloaking woodlands in a soft lime mist.

That was the sight that greeted me when I reached the Suwannee River in early March. Spring was beginning, and the land seemed fresh and happy. The nostalgia of the Old South still lingers in the region. For about 50 miles the trail clings to the riverbank, and it's easy to imagine the little cabins in the moonlight and the little steamers that puffed up and down the tea-colored stream. Any sense of time seems to evaporate.

Long ago, the local Indians held the Suwannee sacred. It was the river's moon, they believed, that put the colors of the rainbow on the earth. Ironically, it was a Pennsylvania native who immortalized it. In 1851 Stephen Foster wrote his song about the old folks at home, "way down upon the Swanee River," and in 1950 a memorial to him was erected at White Springs. This was a popular resort around 1900. Its mineral springs drew the health-conscious from near and far. Cure rheumatism, kidney trouble, even blemishes! Or so the advertisements claimed. At least a dozen hotels accommodated guests, who could watch moving-picture shows in a second-floor room at the bank.

Today even the magnolias along the main street have stooped to time. Yet with its year-round population of 900, the town is the largest on the river and a convenient source of supplies for hikers. I stopped by one day with Margaret Scruggs, a long-time FTA member who used to keep the records, and the town restaurant was serving crisp fried chicken—no franchise here!

At the Stephen Foster State Folk Culture Center, a melody was floating from the 200-foot carillon tower. Amber mist veiled the river, and the countryside seemed as wistful as the song. From the trail, it looked amazingly unspoiled. Cypress roots—furrowed and twisted like an old arthritic hand—spread along the bank between pure white sand beaches, idyllic camping sites. The mist had turned to delicate rain, and the woods to an Impressionist painting. The crisp white of dogwoods and the lime of the cypresses blurred in the dull gray of Spanish moss. Even the vivid hue of the redbuds seemed subdued. Threading through it all was the deep green of resurrection ferns.

Quickly the trail takes on elevation, climbing an ancient dome of limestone. A bluff called Devil's Mountain rises all of 130 feet above the river. Going west, a hiker must cope with lesser heights, ford minor streams, push aside stems of bamboo, and test the sense of balance on cable bridges.

The rain strengthened, and the footing turned slippery, and Margaret and I turned back. It was time for me to head west into the Panhandle. I explored St. Marks National Wildlife Refuge, where salt marshes reach for the horizon and hikers must find boat passage on the St. Marks River. I took a look at the thickets of titi (also called buckwheat tree) in the Apalachicola National Forest—map-and-compass wilderness. My last day in Florida I spent along a stretch proposed in the Gulf Islands National Seashore. When finished, it will complete the existing trail between central Florida and the western tip of the Panhandle. And what better way to end this trip than by watching an anhinga take flight at sunset over the blue waters of the Gulf of Mexico?

The Benton MacKaye Trail

Dark clouds chased our car all the way to the trailhead at Dally Gap. As we parked, the rain began to fall, a drizzle, then a downpour. In the car we finished ham sandwiches and watched the storm slacken. When we set out, the forest had a fresh if sodden beauty. White and pink rhododendron blossoms—past their prime in late June and heavy with water—clung valiantly to their stems. Raindrops shimmered from fern fronds; mossy patches took on the look of brushed velvet in the mist. Spiderwebs tickled our faces. A solitary box turtle stopped nibbling greenery and vanished into its shell as we came up. Gnawed tree trunks on the riverbanks to our right told of the abundance of beavers, once nearly extinct in the area. Here, in Georgia's Cohutta Wilderness, there was no sign of man.

"This is how a forest should look," commented my hiking companion, George Owen. A narrow path threaded its way among tall, dense tulip poplars, hemlocks, and oaks, and occasionally an uprooted one blocked it. We were on the Benton MacKaye Trail, a mountain route—the name rhymes with sky—which wends 78.5 miles across northern Georgia to the Tennessee line.

A United Methodist minister in Atlanta, George is a past president of the Benton MacKaye Trail Association and currently the trail's maintenance supervisor. Opinionated and witty, he was the perfect hiking companion. Except for one thing. He has a wild spirit that manifests itself in his rapid gait. At times I panted and puffed to keep up with him, scrambling over fallen trees and up rain-slick slopes. Though a Floridian by birth, George has developed mountain legs that put many native highlanders to shame. Fortunately, we paused to admire small creatures—a praying mantis swiveling its head alertly, a tiger swallowtail playing tag with a pink blossom. A short downgrade led us to a quiet stream with two mossy stones for crossing. "There are no bridges in the wilderness," George reminded me when I hesitated.

None in the Cohutta Wilderness, but the trail does boast some. One is a 260-foot suspension bridge built by the Forest Service in the mid '70s across the white waters of the Toccoa River. Dark hemlock coves along the banks have become popular for weekend picnics and camping. As on the rest of this trail, however, there are no picnic tables, no paved campgrounds, no shelters. Instead there's the sense of untamed countryside, the essence of the BMT.

"The Benton MacKaye Trail is a remote wilderness footpath that links many wilderness areas," David M. Sherman told me from his National Park Service office in Washington, D.C. "It's one of the most remote in the East." Dave is considered the founding father of this trail, which in part follows the original route mapped by MacKaye for his offspring, the Appalachian Trail. In 1930 the Appalachian Trail Conference chose a more easterly route instead.

MacKaye was a classic Yankee, tall, sharp of feature and wit; a friend called him "tart as a wild apple, sweet as a hickory nut." A principal founder of the Wilderness Society, forester, philosopher and planner, MacKaye devoted most of his 96 years to the efficient and careful use of America's wild lands. He envisioned the Appalachian Trail as a vacation place that even the underpaid or the unpaid—industrial workers, farmers, housewives—could afford.

He proposed his trail in a magazine article in 1921. An avid interest in backpacking and history led Dave Sherman to research MacKaye's letters about the AT in the 1970s. He located original documents wherever he could, even in a Georgia garage. "I noticed," he told me, "that MacKaye's papers had the southern terminus in the Cohutta Mountains, which were very inaccessible in the 1920s. But as I put my maps together, I saw how logical his route was—across the high and more remote western arm of the Blue Ridge."

Such a route, Dave and others believed, would attract hikers from badly overused southern portions of the AT—especially those within a three-hour drive of Atlanta, Asheville, Chattanooga, Greenville, and Knoxville. Dave supervised planning and mapping for the new trail while working for the Georgia Department of Natural Resources. But, he said, "it's the volunteers that made the trail what it is today; they're the ones who've invested 14,000 hours of labor." In 1980 a handful of them formed the BMTA and, with the Forest Service, began construction. "We organized work groups one Saturday each month," George Owen told me. He's proud that the group has missed only one Saturday of work in ten years, and then due to heavy snow.

Marty Dominy, a Georgian in his thirties with Rhett Butler looks, joined the association in 1985. A civil engineer, he quickly earned the title of construction supervisor. One Sunday afternoon in Blue Ridge, Georgia, he showed me the route on his maps. One segment of 160 miles would link the AT's southern terminus at Springer Mountain with Cheoah Dam near the southern tip of the Great Smokies; a second, of 80 miles, would run within the Great Smoky Mountains National Park northeast to Davenport Gap. Fortunately, 95 percent of it would fall on public lands. With the AT, it would form a big lopsided figure 8, allowing a backpacker to hike a 475-mile circuit and return to the starting point without backtracking. It would be the only such opportunity in the region. The BMTA hopes to have all 240 miles complete in 1999; 30-some new miles to go, Marty said, "and we average about 5 miles a year."

Tennessee already has some trails that fit the BMTA guidelines, and a growing membership to help construct linking paths between them. A decision on this segment awaits the completion of an environmental assessment. One of the problems to be ironed out in North Carolina, Marty said, involves bears. As planned, the trail would open up an area currently troubled by poachers, and there're no ranger stations near the route.

I enjoyed the hospitality of BMTA president Ted Reissing and his wife, Kay, one evening in their mountain cabin, where members often relax after work trips. Against a chorus of summer insects, Ted reminisced about his involvement with the BMT and spoke of reasons why people take part in such projects. "One of the major ones, I think, is that all of us want a part of us to live on afterward. Not many of us will be famous enough to be in history books. Kay and I coined the phrase that has become the association's motto: 'We're leaving a footpath for generations to follow.' That's now the logo printed on our T-shirts." I remembered Benton MacKaye's words about caring for the countryside. Such work, he wrote, appeals to instincts of heroism and "is vital in any real protection of 'home and country.' "

*W*ispy threads of Yahoo Falls drop 113 feet beside a "rock house" more than 500 feet long. Hikers savor the cool shade—or rainproof shelter—of such overhangs.

FOLLOWING PAGES: *Autumn-bright slopes of the Cumberland Mountains doze in early morning fog. Here, Daniel Boone National Forest honors the explorer whose Shawnee Indian name—meaning Big Turtle—identifies the trace.*

THE
SHELTOWEE
TRACE

Photographed by Annie Griffiths Belt

*A*h, wilderness! A Boy Scout troop's bridge—pre-knotted in Richmond, Kentucky—proves its strength over a creek at the Turkey Foot Recreation Area, one of numerous popular campground sites along the Sheltowee.

*O*ld-timey skills survive in Sheltowee country. Store-owner Earnest Bush
wields his whittling knife, watched by his granddaughter Megan Caldwell. Pioneer
girls played with cornshuck dolls, prized by grown-up collectors now.

*B*oneset, locally called dog fennel, flanks Florida Trail Association members on their
Presidents' Day weekend backpack trip, a 26-mile trek west of the Kissimmee River.
Two groups set out from opposite points, to meet midway and exchange car keys.
Unique among major trails, the Florida offers its best hiking in winter, the dry season.
Then moderate heat, fewer insects, and abundant migratory waterfowl enhance its
corridor of subtropical vegetation—1,100 miles long, and growing longer.

THE
FLORIDA
TRAIL

Photographed by Medford Taylor

"Wednesday Wonders," volunteers of the FTA's Suncoast chapter, drag a 3,000-pound utility pole to the creek it will span as part of a new footbridge in the Little Manatee River State Recreation Area. Block-and-tackle gear assists the crew: seven men and two women tugging in synchrony with retired electrician Vic Moore.

*F*lorida's marshes, prairies, and swamps support a spectacular flora and fauna, adapted to slight variations of drainage. Woodstorks (right) frequent marshy areas along the northeastern tip of Lake Okeechobee. Breeding habitat to the south has suffered, however, as human activities have disrupted the natural flow of water to the Everglades. In the tropical conditions of Collier-Seminole State Park, a swamp lily raises blossoms four inches wide. At sunset their fragrance intensifies, attracting moths for pollination.

FOLLOWING PAGES: *January's morning light filters through mist and Spanish moss where hardwood trees and saw palmettos line the banks of the Suwannee River. Here, noted the author, "the nostalgia of the Old South still lingers."*

*B*urrowing owls, active for much of the day in the prairies along the Kissimmee
River, often return the curious stares of hikers on the Florida Trail.
Without even taking wing, they busily snap up grasshoppers and other insect prey.

"*The only true 100 percent normal forest is the primeval forest," wrote
Benton MacKaye, father of the Appalachian Trail. This scene reflects the wilderness
advocate's belief. It lies on the route proposed for a new trail in the Great Smoky
Mountains National Park, in North Carolina. Adapting the original plan that
MacKaye proposed for the AT, it would provide an alternative for that popular
trail's most heavily used sections in the southern Appalachians.*

THE
BENTON MACKAYE
TRAIL

Photographed by Robb Kendrick

*B*alancing warily, a hiker gets a drink from the lower cascade of three-tiered
Fall Branch Waterfalls, at the boundary of the Chattahoochee National Forest in Georgia.
Local people often visit this beauty spot after church on Sundays.
Mountain laurel (above), abundant here, usually blossoms in late May, with
rhododendron following a few weeks later. Virginia creeper frames a visitor's discovery:
weathered shells of white-lipped forest snails, common in the region.

*E*ventually the MacKaye Trail should lead trekkers past slopes of moss (give
or take a maple seedling) and beside tumbling waters of the Smokies in North Carolina.
"It promises a true wilderness experience," says Ted Reissing of Atlanta,
who is president of the Benton MacKaye Trail Association. Completion of the trail
by the target date of 1999 will depend on the continued cooperation of the U.S. Forest
and National Park Services, private landowners, and volunteers.

*F*ine *weather favors the author in mountains notorious for some of the world's worst, New Hampshire's Presidentials. Spectacular scenery has drawn hikers there at least since 1819, when Abel Crawford and his son Ethan cleared a footpath to Mount Washington. Persistent popularity now makes it the nation's oldest continuously maintained mountain trail. Gaining on timberline, Tom climbs Crawford Path toward Lakes of the Clouds Hut, at 5,012 feet the highest of the Appalachian Mountain Club's huts.*

THE
NORTHEAST

By Thomas B. Allen

The White Mountains Trails

NEW
HAMPSHIRE

*I*t started easy enough, this trip to the clouds. The trail ascended, impercep-
tibly at first, and the guidebook said the Zealand Falls Hut was only 2.7
miles away. Easy. But now I'm wondering if the book ever makes a mistake. Should it be 3.7 miles? We've been hiking for two hours. . . .

Here in the White Mountain National Forest the Appalachian Mountain
Club maintains a string of eight huts, about a day's hike apart. My wife, Scottie, and I plan to hike to four of them, spending a night in each. We estimate
that in four and a half days we will hike about 25 miles. Not exactly a forced
march, especially without camping equipment. But we are flatlanders, and we
had not taken the measure of the mountains looming around us.

A long avenue of birches, their crowns glowing with October colors,
climbs the trail ahead. After a few turns in the trail, the birches thin out.
Among them are knee-high firs, branches sprinkled with fallen leaves. In the
dappling light these fall-trimmed firs look like stubby Christmas trees. Beside
the ragged shore of a beaver pond the trail rises sharply to a rocky stair leading
to the Zealand Falls Hut. Perched on a granite ledge at 2,700 feet, the hut is our
gateway to timberline. From here on, the way will be ever upward.

The hut is a sturdy cabin with bunks for 36 people, a kitchen, wash-
rooms, and a porch that looks out upon a darkly green forest patched with red
and orange. A path along the ledge leads to the falls: Chill waters flow across
flat, shining stones, dip into shallow pools, then vanish over a steep drop.

We settled in, changing boots for moccasins, making up our bunks (hikers tote sleep sacks or sheets; the huts supply blankets). From the kitchen came
whiffs of dinner. This was being prepared by the hut crew, always spelled
c-r-o-o on hut bulletins. This is one of the tribal customs of the huts, whose history dates from 1888, when the first one was built. The AMC, as the club is usually known, began installing hutmasters in 1906, and ever since they have been
the custodians of trail tradition and mountain lore. Today they're usually col-
lege students and they all have an intense devotion to the mountains. They
learn their specialized skills on the job.

At precisely six o'clock, by the light of gas-powered lamps, we were all
sitting on benches at two long tables. There were about 20 of us: young and
middle-aged couples, a pair of six-year-old boys and their fathers, a one-year-
old making his first hike (in a backpack with a large pocket for diapers), and
some solo hikers who seemed anxious to return to the solitude of the trail.

*C*ool September nights by the Zealand Trail redden hobblebush leaves gnawed
*by caterpillars. The lanky shrub thrives in moist lowland forests, putting down new
roots where looping branches touch the ground—and snare unwary hikers.*

The croo, Chuck Wooster and Paul Blackburn, served the meal, a delicious combination of new and old: fresh-baked bread and a soup made of rice and last night's chicken, spaghetti with tomato sauce, fresh green beans, and dessert bars containing oatmeal left over from breakfast.

Dinner, Chuck told first-time hut guests, is traditionally followed by a "dinner talk." Soon he was talking about mountain plants. Someone mentioned the avenue of birches. White birches, Chuck said. "They're about 80 years old and are nearing the end of their lifespan. They were the pioneer species, after the logging, and as they go the forest will begin to change." What comes next? Balsam fir—those little Christmas trees—and red spruce. Then Chuck took us back to the turn of the century, when part of the trail had been the railbed for logging trains. Relentless logging stripped the Zealand Valley of all but dead and stunted trees and huge piles of discarded branches and tree-tops. Fires swept through often. On the porch, looking out on the blackness of night and forest, I imagined the desolation and marveled at the renewal.

One by one and two by two, we drifted into the coed bunkrooms and, by discreet flashlight, got ready for bed. Lights-out came at 9:30, another tradition. It needed no enforcement.

At 6:30 a.m. Paul strolled into the bunkrooms singing "Pack Up Your Sorrows," first softly and then a bit louder. Precisely at 7 we were all sitting down to new oatmeal and new pancakes, and before 8 we were off for a hut about seven miles away. A sign reminded us that logging still goes on in the valley.

*T*oday's trail took us down to the Crawford Notch, a major north-south route through the mountains. There at the AMC hostel we would meet photographer Ray Gehman, and then the three of us would head up the Crawford Path, the oldest continually used hiking trail in the country. We crossed a brook and entered a bowered stretch of trail, a cool tunnel garnished with the many greens of moss. It climbed trees, carpeted stones, made mysterious mounds and bumps out of logs and roots. The air hung damp and sweet with the moldering scents of woodland passing into winter. We emerged on a steep, rocky hill that swooped down to a sunny field. At the edge of the field, near the highway, stood the hostel. Its walls were New England clapboard, sternly white. Inside, next to the pay phone, was the number for a pizza place. But we made coffee and dug into our supply of trail lunches (mostly cheese and gorp, a mix of nuts and raisins and whatever else that seems healthy and can endure squashing).

Ray's arrival meant a quick switch from hiking to driving, for car shuffling is part of the hut-to-hut adventure. Driving in the mountains gives a perspective to hiking. Roads follow river valleys or mountain passes; trails take the harder, shorter way, ascending to ridges and going from peak to peak.

In 1819 Abel and Ethan Crawford, pioneers of White Mountain tourism, cut their path to the alpine heart of the Presidential Range: 6,288-foot Mount Washington, the highest mountain in New England. In 1840 they made their path a horse trail and Abel, at the age of 74, became the first man to ride to the top of Mount Washington. I thought of him often.

After we had trudged only a few hundred feet, the Crawford Path seemed to be bending almost to the vertical. We ranged farther and farther apart, each of us hiking a pace set by heart and lung, not by will. But the day was clear and sunny, and the cutoff to our next stop was mercifully short.

The last turn, on a ridge 3,800 feet up the southern flank of Mount Pierce, surprised us with the first view of Mizpah Spring Hut. Under a sharply pitched roof was a huge building, big enough for 60 hikers. Ravens strutted in the meadow around the hut. Sun poured through its tall southern windows.

That night, after dinner under bulbs lit by solar-powered batteries, Annie Hanaway came out of the kitchen holding up a candy wrapper left by a hiker. "You've got to think beyond the end of your hand," she said. "Tonight's dinner talk is going to be about garbage." We looked at each other uncomfortably. "I thought you ought to know about all the kinds," Annie continued. "We haul out plastics, tinfoil, meat scraps, and sweepings. We put the stuff in bags and put on packboards and haul it out. An AMC van picks it up at a trailhead on the highway. Food scraps, vegetable peelings, we compost for fertilizer." Ashes go into barrels to be lifted out at season's end, along with propane tanks, by helicopter. (A chopper also brings major supplies twice a season. Fresh food, lashed to towering packboards, comes in by croo foot.)

Mizpah gets its name from a biblical meeting place marked by a heap of stones. Until now, we had been watching for painted blazes on trees or occasional boulders. Ahead, winding upward beyond the trees, we would be on the watch for cairns—unmortared piles of stones.

The day began under a sky full of glory, brilliantly blue with scraps of wildly billowing clouds. On the Crawford Path again, we walked at timberline. For a while the trail followed a crest so high and sharp that it seemed to be a passage through the sky. "I felt as if I was walking along the top of the world," Scottie said later. "I could look in any direction and see mountains, mountains. I saw farther than I had ever seen." At times the trail dipped from the crest. We would scrabble along a rocky slope to a ridge, hike along a tilted stretch, then scrabble again. Some slopes were so smooth and steep that they demanded a new verb in the guidebook—"After slabbing to the left. . . ." I define slabbing as the act of leaning in toward a slope, ready to use your hands as you shuffle along a narrow foothold.

While slabbing, I slipped on a smooth rock and hurtled off the ledge. The weight of my backpack flipped me into an involuntary somersault and I landed face-up—on something soft and bouncy. Later I learned another new word: This stuff was krummholz, a patch of matted, stunted black spruce and balsam fir. These little trees that caught me may have been 70 to 150 years old.

Krummholz marks the border between timberline and alpine tundra, with its mosses, sedges, lichens, and tiny flowers. A foot coming down on a tundra meadow can wipe out a fragile life that was a century in growing.

We would learn more about that life at our next stop, Lakes of the Clouds Hut, at 5,012 feet the highest—and, with bunks for 90 hikers, the largest. A stone building wedged into the southern shoulder of Mount Washington, this hut evolved from a shelter built following the deaths of two hikers here in a storm on a June day in 1900. In any month, fierce storms can suddenly swirl down from the summit, where the temperature has dropped to 47°F below zero and where winds have reached a world-record 231 miles per hour. Even as we straggled into the hut, the day was turning dark and rainy. The great hulk of Washington was a dim white shadow against the thickening sky.

Up a misty trail from the hut, above one of the two small lakes nestled there, June Hammond of the AMC research department was hurrying with her work, collecting clouds. For this she needs clouds but not rain. "If your eyelashes get wet, you know it's a great day for cloud sampling," she remarked. Her lashes were wet and so was her hair, which was being ruffled by winds being clocked at 12 miles per hour.

The cloud trap is rigged to a vane that keeps it pointed into the wind. Winds pass through baffles that filter out water drops hanging in the air. Only a wisp of cloud enters the collection chamber, where moisture adheres to Teflon strands and runs through tubes down to a small bottle. By such sampling, June explained, researchers can analyze the moisture before it condenses naturally. The study helps track the spread and intensity of acid rain.

AMC researchers help Forest Service personnel guard an endangered plant, Robbins' cinquefoil. Its only remaining natural colony is here. Its protectors have diverted a stretch of the Crawford Path, edged it with a low wall of stone, and posted warning signs. Some plants have been moved to suitable sites nearby. At one of these, balanced on stones, I crouched down and through a magnifying glass examined a plant that could grow on a dime. Its yellow flowers had faded away, but its leaves showed red and faint yellow.

June, who spoke of the cinquefoil as if it were a kitten, said, "It likes a gravelly spot like this." Among the pebbles around it I noticed a rock about as long as a middle finger. How lucky, I said, that the plant had a rock to shield it from northerly winds. "We put the rock there," June confessed. "But, well, it *could* have been right there anyway, couldn't it?"

At every hut, the day's weather forecast is posted at 8 a.m. With our party, hikers in ponchos and yellow slickers crowded around the Lakes of the Clouds bulletin board: gusts to 60 miles per hour at the top of Washington. For us, there would be no hike on the summit trail. Leaning into a steady, drenching wind, swathed in driving cloud, we headed for the ridge trail around the western shoulder of the mountain. I could see only ten feet ahead. Again and again Ray and Scottie and I lost sight of one another.

On an exposed ridge, winds whipped away the cloud cocoons around us, but brought a torrent of rain from higher strata. We slogged across Mount Jefferson, stumbled down to a cloud-filled ravine, and groped our way from cairn to cairn. Whoever was first would set out to what looked like a cairn. If the shape was one of those blessed works of art, the finder would shout, and slowly two figures would make their way forward. When all three assembled, one of us would head out and the search would begin again.

In early afternoon the sky began to clear. By then, the trail had disappeared under an endless chaos of rocks—piled and scattered, large and small, sharp-edged and bare, smooth and lichen-covered, jiggling beneath each wary step. Geologists say that frost and ice cracked this jumble off from bedrock. I think these devilish rocks came from a much deeper domain.

Madison Spring Hut finally came into sight far away and far below. We still had countless quivering piles of rocks to clamber over. But our longest day and longest hike—about seven miles in the guidebook, about twenty in my imagination—was nearly over.

Next day, in sodden boots but in sunshine, we practically strolled down to trees and a parking lot. As I took my last step out of the mountains, Scottie told me to turn around. I had missed a yellow sign on a tree. "Try this trail," the U.S. Forest Service warned, "*only* if you are in top physical condition, well clothed and carrying extra clothing and food. Many have died above timberline from exposure. Turn back at first sign of bad weather."

The Long Trail

VERMONT

*A*ll night it rained, and the rain was still coming down this morning when I started out. Most of the trail is a gully. When my backpack brushes an overhanging branch, I get a double lash of rain, along with some sodden leaves. Yes, it's foliage season in Vermont, but right now my head is bowed to the rain—and my left boot. After 20-odd years of faithful service, the boot has sprung open at the toes. With each step it's squirting water.

That was the day I climbed to a scrap of arctic-alpine tundra on Camel's Hump. The 4,083-foot peak is a gem of the Long Trail, which follows the mountainous spine of Vermont for 265 miles from the Massachusetts line to the Canadian border. The trail runs from crest to crest, and by long tradition usually goes straight up without switchbacks. The guidebook warns that it is "steep, boggy, and rugged." It is all that, and worth every step as well.

The Green Mountain Club, founded in 1910 to build a "footpath in the wilderness," blazed its first trail—from Mount Mansfield to Camel's Hump—within a year. Then, all of Vermont's high peaks were wild. Today, Camel's Hump is the only one untouched by ski lifts or other human invention. I climbed the last steep slope to its bare summit in late afternoon. The rains were gone, but clouds clung to the still air like wraiths. The only color was the green of lichens on the gray rocks. The only sound was the *pip pit* of three or four water pipits that dipped in and out of the clouds. I felt an exhilaration of solitude.

The pipits seemed to follow me as I groped along the trail, marked by red-bordered white blazes painted on the rocks. The trail spiraled around to keep feet off patches of dark earth. Here in autumn sleep were fragile, ground-hugging arctic-alpine plants that are relics of the ice ages. The trail wound along the crest, across jumbled rocks, and finally down to the woods surrounding Montclair Glen Lodge, one of the cabins that the Green Mountain Club has strung along the trail. In the fading light a furry gray shadow darted across the path. A coyote, I decided; more likely here than wolves.

Beyond the last two streams of the day I saw an oil-lamp glowing in a window of the cabin. Jeff, the caretaker, was playing cribbage with Rick, who was walking the length of the Long Trail. They hardly looked up. People do not go into the wilderness to chat. My backpack was soaked, but my sleeping bag and other clothes were dry in plastic bags. I changed, and made soup and coffee on an alcohol-fueled stove. The game ended, and Jeff and I talked a little. "We get a lot of day hikers in the fall," he said. "Not so many backpackers." I told him about the furry shadow. He nodded and said, "Saw a moose once. Came right up to the window." Jeff and Rick started another game, and I crawled into my sleeping bag.

Next morning, in bright sunshine, hiking near a waterfall roaring with yesterday's rain, I saw a peregrine falcon on a high branch, eyes on the pool below the fall. I hoped to see it dive for prey, but it flew away. Falcons, victims of insecticides in the food chain, had disappeared from the Green Mountains in the 1960s. Today the state has at least seven pairs, descended from captive stock, and one pair nests on the Great Cliff of Mount Horrid, where a chunk of bedrock rises more than 600 feet near the Long Trail.

In an hour or so I reached my car at the end of a dirt road. Today I would be slackpacking, a term I found in a trail shelter's log. A slackpacker arranges to be dropped at a trailhead by someone who will park the car a day's hike away. Needing no camping gear, the hiker carries a slack pack. My slackpacking began at the top of Mount Mansfield, the highest point in Vermont and a mountain claimed by civilization: toll road, ski lifts, TV antennas. But for two and a half miles the trail follows the summit ridge, which is a national natural landmark and mostly clear of unnatural clutter. Here in dazzling sunshine I could look at an alpine world I had only seen dimly on Camel's Hump.

Viewed from a distance, Mount Mansfield is supposed to resemble the profile of a man with a stub nose and a jutting chin. (Imagine him in a barber's chair looking at the ceiling.) The alpine meadow is between the Nose (at 4,062 feet) and the Chin (the highest point, at 4,393 feet).

Already the meadow was in winter. The white flowers of the mountain sandwort had come and gone, but tiny spots of blue hid in the dark green mats of alpine bilberries. Spikes of brownish sedge thrust amid the rocks. A plant called Labrador tea covered hummocks of soil with leathery brown leaves.

A young man and woman were walking toward me from the Chin. When I asked about the trail down, he said, "It's not for us." She nodded. I walked on until I was looking down a cliff, almost straight down. For a moment I wondered where the trail went. And then I saw the white blazes far below. Thinking about close shaves, I carefully made my way off the Chin.

The 2.3-mile hike down from the summit is vertically equivalent to traveling about 1,500 miles southward from the arctic of Hudson Bay. In a few yards I had left the glittering gray rocks for a thin stand of balsam fir and red spruce. About half a mile down, amid a denser cluster of fir and spruce, a long, narrow log cabin stood on a rocky shelf. This was Taft Lodge, oldest and largest of the trail's cabins.

Farther down, birches appeared, their bright yellow leaves still clinging to black branches. In this zone, Steve Weber, Taft's caretaker, was digging shallow trenches. He said he was draining water from the treadway, the part of the trail that feet step on. He pointed to a log half-buried diagonally across the treadway. "That's a waterbar," he said. "It diverts water off the trail and into the trench. With all this rain, the trenches were filling up with silt." As he cleared a trench, backed-up water flowed downslope and disappeared into the leaf litter. Without such maintenance a trail becomes an ever-deepening gully. Trail keepers estimate that in some places a hiker in just four steps walks a reach of trail that took a week to build.

I finished my hike to the highway and car in a forest aflame with the reds and golds of sugar maples and beech. Down from the arctic, I was back in a Vermont of swirling colors.

A few days later I was backpacking again, along the middle stretch of the trail. In late afternoon I hiked down to the three-sided Sucker Brook Shelter, which opened to a bog bristling with saplings. As soon as the sun dropped behind the ridge, an autumn chill filled the little valley. After a last cup of coffee, I unrolled my sleeping bag and crawled in far enough to cover my head.

Suddenly, at some dark hour, I was awake. *It was a moaning. A deep, insistent moaning.* Confused, thinking that another hiker was in some terrible trouble up the trail, I fumbled for my flashlight and shone it into blackness.

The moaning stopped, but something was crashing around in the saplings. I skimmed the beam across the bog—and caught a pair of red-orange eyes. *Bear*! No. The shape . . . two shapes . . . took form. I played the beam around them. Moose. Two of them. The crashing started again, and they vanished into the dark.

*T*he southern third of the Long Trail—102.5 miles beginning at the state line—coincides with the younger Appalachian Trail. At Sherburne Pass, near Rutland, the two trails part, the Appalachian veering east to New Hampshire, the Long Trail continuing northward. "We joke that the AT is a side trail," one of the field supervisors told me.

On the pass is the Inn at Long Trail, which accepts mail and parcels for hikers. On a table near the front door is the Hiker's Box, where the wealthy or the weary can jettison unneeded supplies and the poor or foolish can pick up more stuff to carry. I contributed a package of noodles. The Hiker's Box was the idea of innkeeper Kyran McGrath, who over the years has classified hikers as the rich and the poor. "I can tell when they pick up their packages," he told me. "The rich hikers go through the package and, realizing by now what even an ounce of extra weight means, leave a lot in the Hiker's Box. The poor upgrade their rations from what the rich leave behind."

Near the inn is one of nine ski resorts on the Long Trail. In many places along the trail, civilization lurks at the edge of wilderness, waiting to pounce. Once, where a hillside was being cleared to make way for several houses, I clambered over trees that had been felled across the trail. At the next shelter I read in the log the experience of hikers just before me: "Nearly bulldozed . . . had to dodge an enormous boulder rolling down freshly torn-up hillside."

"When the LT was conceived and built, all the land was private," as Harry T. Peet, Jr., then executive director of the Green Mountain Club, explained. "The landowners were very generous. We made agreements through handshakes rather than having anything written down. Hiking and downhill skiing coexisted very well, but skiing areas are now beginning to be year-round resorts. Since the mid-1970s most of them have been attempting to get into summer activities. They've gone into real estate."

So, defensively, has the club. In 1987 it made its first land purchase in the northern tier, where, for about 38 miles, the route passes over private property. The club, hoping to buy a 1,000-foot-wide corridor, is looking for fund-raisers as well as trail maintenance crews.

I needed only to hike up Jay Peak to see the clash of interests. From the south, the way to the 3,861-foot ski slope is a winding, windswept span of the trail, a climb through birch and spruce, rock and scrub. Then the legs and cables of a tramway lift march into view. Here is the raw rock where the top of the mountain was blasted away to make room for the lift and a restaurant.

From Jay Peak the Long Trail winds about ten miles to the Canadian border. The trees close in and the path is easy, untouched by any human marks but footprints. I watch a single birch leaf fall, then walk on. At last I find a metal shaft that looks like a miniature Washington Monument. This is Line Post 592, set up in 1907 in fulfillment of what the marker identifies as *Treaty of Washington 1842.* Beyond is a boundary come to green life, an endless vista of neighborly nationhood. The swath is twenty feet wide—ten feet of cleared land contributed by each country—and it rolls on, wherever there is forest, from Maine to Alaska. At Line Post 592, the world looked vividly hopeful in every direction.

The Potomac Heritage Trail

PENNSYLVANIA

MARYLAND
WASHINGTON, D.C.

VIRGINIA

A hiking trail courses a map like a line that solves a connect-the-dots puzzle. The line starts somewhere, passes a pond, climbs a peak, dips into a valley . . . and finally ends somewhere. Not so the Potomac Heritage National Scenic Trail. It starts and ends at nowhere, a puzzle not yet solved. But it wanders through countryside and cityside I have known for years, and I enjoy working on the puzzle. The trail's dots—parks, capital shrines, landmarks of three states—sprinkle a rumpled terrain from Pennsylvania into Virginia. Some of the dots are connected along the old towpath of the Chesapeake and Ohio Canal. Other dots mark urban bike paths or abandoned railbeds, wistfully awaiting a connecting line. Part dream, part walkable, the PHT has been as much an endurance test for planners as for hikers.

I found this out while hiking with Thurston Griggs, president of the Potomac Heritage Trail Association, one of the puzzle solvers. Today his quest has taken him to the hills of western Maryland. We cross a farm field awaiting the spring plow. Ahead somewhere is a path to a marsh and a way into the trail system of a state forest. "There's a more direct route across another farm," says Thurston. "I got a nice letter from a farmer who said we could use it. He also told me about his bulls. So we don't go there."

We spend the day driving from dot to dot, then checking out segments of proposed route. We walk the shoulders of roads, follow a buried pipeline right-of-way, skirt two working strip mines, thread our way through the parking lot of a shopping mall. This is no wilderness path, but, by a 1983 Act of Congress, it may become part of the national system. The Congressional vision of the Potomac Heritage Trail—"a corridor of approximately 704 miles"—is sweeping: from Virginia's Smith Point on Chesapeake Bay, through the District of Columbia and Maryland, to Pennsylvania's wild and twisty Youghiogheny River and—by way of the 70-mile Laurel Highlands Trail—to Conemaugh Gorge near Johnstown, site of the notorious flood of 1889.

Scottie and I have lived for years near the heart of the trail, the C & O Canal, which begins in the Georgetown section of Washington. The towpath, where mules pulled the canal boats, is ideal for strollers, joggers, cyclists, kids with dogs, and young parents with baby packs snuggled to chests. The canal is a waterway for canoeists or, in winter, an ice-skating rink. For years Scottie and I brought our children here; now we bring our grandchildren.

On one long-distance excursion, we introduced our six-year-old grandson, Aaron, to the canal's Paw Paw Tunnel, a mile north of Milestone 156, at Sorrel Ridge. The 3,118-foot tunnel, a monument to manual labor and contractor bankruptcy, was begun with picks and spades and blasting powder in 1836 and not finished until 1850. Outside the tunnel, Aaron had his first-ever drink of water from a hand pump. Then, a fearless fan of ghost stories, he plunged into the darkness. Along one side of the brick-lined tunnel ran a railed wooden boardwalk, like one the mules had used. About a third of the way through, Aaron's flashlight picked out a small hole in the wall. I thought I saw a cable in it. Puzzled, I reached in and Aaron exclaimed, "It's a snake!" Stirred by my touch, a tightly coiled blacksnake lifted its head into the beam, giving me a memorable scare and Aaron a wonderful tale that would always be his.

Our snake-in-the-tunnel adventure shows what the PHT does so well: It gives its walkers experiences that combine the wild and the historic, the realm of nature and the works of America's past and present.

Sometimes this is an uneasy coexistence. A few days after our spring hike, Thurston called to say that the owner of one of the strip mines had withdrawn permission for the trail to cross his land. About four more miles of highway and streets would have to be added to the proposed route.

When I discussed this with David M. Sherman of the National Park Service, godfather of the trail, he nodded philosophically. Because Congress has decreed that the Federal Government cannot acquire land for the trail, its champions must scrounge, make do, and endure rebuffs. "We have to work with what is there," said Dave. "This has to be a grassroots effort."

Talking enthusiastically of trail sections here and to come, he pulled out his working map of the PHT. Striped lines mark potential routes like the one Thurston had been scouting. Broken lines show dreams for the future. One, in Pennsylvania, is a side trail to Fort Necessity, where on July 3, 1754, a French and Indian force attacked and defeated a young, inexperienced George Washington. Dave's finger traced the solid lines showing segments already in existence. Here's the new, surprisingly wild ten-mile river trail that sometimes passes under the shadow of the traffic-clogged Capital Beltway. And there's the hike-or-bike Mount Vernon Trail. It runs from 88-acre Theodore Roosevelt Island—a wilderness isle in the Potomac, opposite the Kennedy Center for the Performing Arts—to Washington's home 18 miles downriver.

"Now there's something you really should see," he said. He pointed to the striped line for Virginia's W&OD Railroad Regional Park. This is 100 feet wide, 45 miles long, and a potential component of the PHT system. One end is in a suburban neighborhood of modest brick homes. For now the other is in horse country at the edge of the Blue Ridge, about nine miles from the Appalachian Trail. The park follows the former railbed of the Washington & Old Dominion Railroad, which impatient passengers used to call the Virginia Creeper. "This trail is really going to surprise you," Dave promised.

A few days later, Scottie and I sampled a stretch of Virginia's skinniest park. Pedaling along a paved path, we passed under superhighways, skirted warehouses and shopping centers, dodged joggers and Frisbee tossers, and cut across a baseball outfield. "It's like a big backyard," said Scottie as we racked the bikes on our car. So are quite a few miles of the Potomac Heritage Trail. It links the wilderness past with an American landscape that, for better or for worse, is occupied by civilization.

*D*ay's trek done, hikers bask outside Galehead Hut. Helicopter drops and hiked-in produce
ensure "hospitality in high places" — an Appalachian Mountain Club motto. Overlooking
the Pemigewasset Wilderness, Galehead ranks as most isolated of eight way stations.

FOLLOWING PAGES: Lakes of the Clouds Hut and namesake tarns sprawl across
rocky Bigelow Lawn, a gateway to the eastern states' most extensive alpine tundra zone.

THE
WHITE MOUNTAINS
TRAILS

Photographed by Raymond Gehman

*H*ikers' icon signals the junction of Crawford Path and Westside Trail, en route to Madison Spring Hut. Soupy weather commonly turns the rocky mountain way into a cairn-to-cairn grope; wind and sudden snow can pose mortal danger even in July.

Tiny Pleiad Lake mirrors a skyful of autumn blaze near Middlebury. From peak to gorge, tundra to fern garden, silent wood to glitzy ski run, Vermont's Green Mountains unfold in unexpected variety on the Long Trail's 265-mile route.

FOLLOWING PAGES: Chanting hikers from Montreal dance the chill away on Camel's Hump—October snow and ice have balked their annual trek to the summit.

THE LONG TRAIL

Photographed by Pete Souza

*T*urning their backs on civilization, hikers pause at sunset beneath Belvidere
Mountain's old fire tower. The peak's shadow centers their view eastward to the
White Mountains. Conceived in 1910 as a "footpath in the wilderness," the strenuous
Long Trail—still almost devoid of switchbacks and such—suggests Vermonters'
own self-reliance. Yet human enterprise has transformed their landscapes. Once heavily
logged, Belvidere Mountain went on to yield most of the country's asbestos
in the 1950s. By then, a burgeoning ski industry was claiming other peaks. The state's
highest, Mount Mansfield bristles with lift towers and antennas. But designation
as a national natural landmark protects a fragile summit ridge, ice-clad by September.

*S*liced veggies become still life at Montclair Glen Lodge, near Camel's Hump.
Offering shelter only, Green Mountain Club huts follow traditions far more spartan than
the Appalachian Mountain Club's. Hikers pack in food, fuel, and sleeping gear.

*M*ule-powered barge on the Chesapeake and Ohio Canal recalls the heyday of westward expansion. Canal boats once linked Washington's tidewater port of Georgetown with hilly Cumberland, Maryland, 184 miles up the Potomac River and gateway to the Ohio Valley. Though the Baltimore & Ohio Railroad soon rendered it obsolete, the canal operated for nearly a century, from 1828 to 1924. Today, its working lift locks, tidy lockhouses, and period-garbed interpreters enhance a tableau central to the region's heritage.

THE
POTOMAC HERITAGE
TRAIL

Photographed by Joel Sartore

*C*arefree paddlers take to the C & O Canal within view of Georgetown University's Healy Hall, its spire soaring above lush foliage. Hardwood stands watered by the Potomac offer shady relief during the capital's humid summers, and tranquillity in any season. Swamp and marsh enrich nature's mix on 88-acre Theodore Roosevelt Island, where John Wall (left) and Amos Lynch pass an afternoon angling for perch.

FOLLOWING PAGES: *Jets scream over Gravelly Point, near Washington National Airport. Historic sites and riparian preserves vary the mood on the Mount Vernon Trail.*

"This is just a national shrine," declares Lee Embrey, on dawn patrol
at Mount Vernon. "You have to protect it with everything you have." Dedication
runs in the family: His father guarded George Washington's riverside estate
for 40 years; the junior Embrey first reported for work in 1956.

*A*cross Devils Lake, East Bluff blushes. Daylight striking traces of iron oxide
in the rocky heights casts this sunset bonus on Wisconsin's Ice Age Trail. In the Midwest,
national scenic trails follow the footsteps of Indians and explorers, pioneers and poets.
Natural wonders abound along the way: palisades, pine forests, glacial lakes.
The largest of these, Lake Superior, moved Longfellow to write: ". . . the evening sun . . . /
Left upon the level water / One long track and trail of splendor. . . ."

THE
MIDWEST

By Scott Thybony

The Ice Age Trail

WISCONSIN

Meltwater cascades from a retreating glacier as massive tongues of ice waste away on the horizon. A braided stream drains southward behind a great woolly mammoth lumbering along near the edge of the ice. I'm standing in front of a mural in the Ice Age Visitor Center of Northern Kettle Moraine State Forest, in Wisconsin. Looking out the window, I can see the same setting fifteen thousand years later: The gray-white world where mammoths roamed has given way to green farmlands and grazing cows.

The visitor center stands on a ridge formed when two major lobes of the advancing ice sheet collided. As the ice melted, it left in its wake a pitted landscape broken by serpentine ridges. From the observation deck I look across glaciated terrain. Its hills and hummocks have a soft flow to them like ocean swells. And somewhere across the valley runs the Ice Age Trail, hidden in a maze of ridges and spurs. When completed, this national scenic trail will meander for a thousand miles across the state of Wisconsin.

With my wife, Sandy, and our eight-year-old son, Erik, I plan to join the trail near the town of Kewaskum and follow it north about thirty miles to the historic village of Greenbush. This route will give us a close-up look at the legacy of the great continental ice sheet, and Erik will have his first experience of backpacking and camping overnight.

At the trailhead, we feel a sense of expectancy. The path winds into a thicket of smooth sumac, a shrub that likes dry soil, at the base of a steep ridge. We shoulder our packs and follow the trail uphill. We're climbing an esker, a winding ridge of sediment deposited by meltwater rushing through an ice tunnel underneath a glacier. Some of these run for miles. Steep and gravelly, quick to dry out after rain, they're natural trail routes.

Much of this esker has been left wooded, a ribbon of forest across a lived-in landscape. Trees screen us from farmhouses and cultivated fields. Our links with the rural countryside are distant sounds—a tractor driven by a farmer taking advantage of good weather, the hollow ring of a church bell, and the hum of faraway cars.

At a grassy clearing we stop for a break. Just after Labor Day, the landscape is so green that it's hard to imagine arctic conditions here. Erik looks across the valley, wondering how high the ice might have stood. I point to clouds drifting several thousand feet above us. "Try to imagine," I tell him, "a sheet of ice so thick it would reach the bottom of those clouds." More than

*D*uckweed, ostrich fern, spruce, and red maple screen Mondeaux Flowage in Chequamegon National Forest. Wisconsin's Ice Age Trail passes this way on its serpentine course along the terminal moraine left by an ice sheet fifteen thousand years ago.

a mile thick: so thick, in fact, that its weight depressed the earth's surface at least a hundred feet—the distance it has rebounded to date.

Clues that helped 19th-century geologists relate these farmlands to the great ice mass were boulders called erratics. The moving ice sheet sheared the old landscape to bedrock, carrying with it billions of tons of stone. Some of these boulders ended up hundreds of miles from their place of origin. Pioneers called them "lost rocks" because they were obviously different from the local dolomite. Farmers cleared them from their fields and used them for fences or foundations. I've seen a photograph of an immense erratic as tall as a man, and am hoping to find one like it.

O ur hike takes on its own gentle rhythm as we cross knob and swale terrain. Here masses of rock debris have left a lumpy landscape; the trail dips and rises as it winds through the trees. Although several runners have jogged past, the land favors an ambling gait. Even the feel of the trail underfoot is gentle, varying between moss and sand and gravel. Meltwater had sorted its load of sediment, and left some areas with better soil than others.

At times the trees are so thick the trail becomes a deep trench cutting through the green world. Then it crosses clearings full of light where grass grows thick and tall. But crews regularly mow a wide swath to keep the trail open. We've never hiked a mowed trail before, and Sandy approves of it: "This is the way hikes should be."

This hummocky terrain is pocked with steep-walled depressions called kettles, distinctive features of the area. They formed when buried masses of ice melted, causing the overlying glacial debris to slump and collapse. Many are dry, but some hold water. The larger kettles form lakes several miles wide; the smaller ones are about the right size to hold one of the giant beavers that lived here during the Ice Age. These animals grew larger than most black bears of today—about seven feet long, weighing perhaps 500 pounds.

Crossing a road, we hike a short distance farther into a forest of hickory and oak. We pitch our tent near a wooden trail shelter, and start a smoky fire to drive away the mosquitoes. We had hoped to escape them, but the weather has remained warm with lots of rain. A farmer had warned me: "They've been coming up thick." They're a novelty to Erik, who's used to ski outings. Swatting mosquitoes, he says, "I thought it was going to be snowy."

The Ice Age Trail begins on the Minnesota border at the St. Croix Dalles, a dramatic gorge cut by glacial floods. For most of its length, it tends to follow an irregular ridge called a terminal moraine. This marks the greatest extent of the last major glacial advance. The trail runs east through a national forest, then drops south through glacier-worked farmlands into naturalist's country—past the site of John Muir's boyhood home, through Aldo Leopold's sand counties—to the Baraboo Range.

Here the ice sheet pushed its way over the eastern hills, leaving a moraine that diverted a river and plugged its gorge. A lake formed between two extensions of the glacier. Indians of the region called it Spirit Lake, a name the pioneers changed to Devils Lake. Here, perhaps, the track of the glacier is most easily traced. The moraine, deposited fifteen thousand years ago, drapes across hills of quartzite formed more than a billion years earlier. Dark pines grow from the talus slopes, next to deciduous trees that cover the moraine with a lighter shade of green. To the east, the softer contours of the glacier-scoured terrain contrast with the rugged pre-glacial land.

From Devils Lake the trail loops to the South Kettle Moraine, then swings north to end on the shore of Green Bay. Several hikers have walked the length of the route, even though only half of it has been completed. Each year volunteers build new sections as rights-of-way are acquired.

"Through time, it's like a river that meanders and cuts a new channel," says Gary Werner, a county coordinator for the Ice Age Park & Trail Foundation. Public and private support runs strong, he adds: "Many of the landowners are enthusiastic, especially in townships settled by Norwegians who brought with them a tradition of ski trails." He is confident the trail will be completed within a matter of years.

When I discussed it with Governor Tommy G. Thompson, he was enthusiastic too: "The trail runs through the best ice age topography in the country. Whether for research or recreation, it's all there." He stressed the need for a strong partnership of government, private corporations, and volunteer labor. Wisconsin now matches funds raised in the private sector. "If you get private involvement," he said, "you have much better chance of success."

As evening cools on the Ice Age Trail, mosquitoes finally quiet down. The only sounds are falling hickory nuts ricocheting from limb to limb, and a squirrel arguing with a blue jay.

Next morning we head north, passing an abandoned farm with a tumbled stone fence. It was built of erratics, but most are fairly small. I'm beginning to think the larger ones have been hauled away for rural lawn ornaments. We stop at an overgrown orchard to pick apples—mementos of families who struggled to farm these marginal lands.

Forest is reclaiming its own, but in some areas we find groves planted in rows as straight as furrows. Once, as the trail breaks into the open, we find ourselves following an esker across a farmer's field. Hay, rolled and baled, lies stacked along the ridge. "They're big pieces of shredded wheat!" shouts Erik. He discards his pack, scrambles on top of a roll, and jumps from one to another down the row.

We skirt a series of lakes and marshes. There's a northern feel to these waters, so cold and clear. When the skies open above a calm kettle lake, clouds drift in reversed beauty across the blue surface. Nearby a few sugar maples are edged in yellow, just beginning to change. Scattered sunlight sifts through the green canopy, prefiguring the leaves that will fall in the coming weeks. From somewhere above comes the honk of a solitary goose heading south.

The map calls our route a terminal moraine, but a geologist had told me there're more eskers on it than anything else. The Parnell Esker reaches a height of 35 feet, and at a high vantage point an observation tower takes us above the trees for a spectacular view of the North Kettle Moraine. Trees mark the course of the glacier ridges we've followed. To the east stretches a fine pastoral landscape: green fields, red barns, silos, church steeples. It's Norman Rockwell country, and I'm glad to discover it still exists.

We make our last camp in a deep hollow next to a dry kettle. Trees stand tall and thick, allowing little undergrowth. Stepping outside the tent at dawn, I see two white-tailed deer standing on a high esker above camp.

The last leg of the hike takes us to Greenbush and its Old Wade House, a historic stagecoach inn, now restored. After stowing my pack and changing into a clean shirt, I join a tour of the premises. Our guide, in the cotton cap and full skirts of the 1850s, leads us across the grounds. I notice an ice-tumbled boulder about the size of a giant beaver. It's a beautiful erratic, the largest one I've seen since we started out. The guide looks puzzled when I point to it and ask what the locals call it. "We call them rocks," she answers matter-of-factly. "And we don't like them. As kids we had to pick them out of the fields."

The North Country Trail: Michigan

MICHIGAN

Gale winds strike the point at Grand Marais where parka-clad residents huddle in twos and threes. They've left the shelter of their homes to watch storm waves explode over the beacon at the end of the breakwater. I stand watch with them, dodging spray and thinking twice about continuing a hike along the North Country Trail.

Three days earlier, I had joined an old friend, Scott Milzer, about forty miles to the west in Pictured Rocks National Lakeshore. We planned to backpack along the most dramatic stretch of the trail as it skirts Lake Superior in Michigan's Upper Peninsula. When completed, this national scenic trail will be the longest marked footway in the country, running 3,200 miles from Lake Champlain in New York to the plains of North Dakota.

We had parked at Miners Castle, a local landmark, and loaded our packs with what felt like enough trail mix to last all winter. I was about to add a smoked whitefish to the food bag when Scott reminded me this was hunting season in black bear country. Every surly bear for miles would be sniffing its way to camp. Reluctantly, I left this local delicacy behind.

The weather was threatening, so we tied rain gear to the outside of our packs. After climbing a steep escarpment, we passed old fields and second-growth woods of beech and maple that screened the lake from view. The trail kept veering toward shore, as if drawn by the emptiness of open water, and we could sense the presence of the lake. Soft light from the water glanced up through the trees on the left; hard sunlight pierced the canopy on the right.

Soon the pathway reached the rim where sheer rock walls fell into the grip of the green waters below. The largest freshwater lake in the world spread before us as far as the eye could follow. We were standing on top of the Pictured Rocks, which form a rampart 15 miles long and reach heights of 200 feet. Rust reds and yellows stain the massive sandstone face, in contrast to the green trees bristling from the rim. This colorful scarp had been noted by French explorers as early as 1659, but the Chippewa had known it long before. They had passed through the area on their seasonal rounds, leaving offerings of tobacco to spirits found at the storm-weathered rocks.

The trail hugged the rim as we continued northeast. Our route took us through mixed hardwoods and evergreens, each stand changing the feel of the trail underfoot from packed sand to springy duff. In mid-September, color had begun to mark the change of seasons, and in places newly fallen maple leaves carpeted the path in yellows and reds.

Before long we came to a stream, Mosquito River. The name had an ominous hum to it, but Scott had come prepared. Driving over Slapneck Creek on the way up had inspired him to buy heavy-duty repellent. We crossed the wooden footbridge without incident—not a mosquito in sight or hearing.

As we rounded the massive headland of Grand Portal Point, the flash of wet paddles 200 feet below caught our attention. Two kayakers were navigating the sea arch that perforates the cliff. Not far beyond, we made camp. Scott heated coffee on a camp stove and talked about Ernest Hemingway, a fitting topic for an English major turned commercial fisherman. Scott's image of Upper Peninsula types had come straight from the Nick Adams stories. "I was hoping against hope," he said, "to find a bunch of guys with big leather boots laced up to their knees, wearing jodhpurs, smoking pipes, and carrying wicker creels. All I saw today was a guy in a rented backpack."

Early next morning, I strolled the beach as blue waters lapped at the base of Chapel Rock, a weathered sandstone monolith. Waves of the ancestral lake—fed by the melting ice sheet—had eroded deep-socketed windows forty feet above the present water level. On top stood a solitary white pine that appeared to grow from bare caprock, with roots poised in midair; when supporting rock collapsed, enough roots had held to secure it on the inland side.

That tree was a reminder of the magnificent stands once found throughout the north woods. They were lost in a few decades of clear-cutting. "I've never seen in all my life such country," a Grand Marais lumberjack recalled before his death in 1948. "No eye in this generation has ever seen such trees. . . . You could look straight up to the sky for more than a hundred feet and see those trees, straight as the barrel of a gun aimin' at the sky."

At camp a red squirrel clung to a lesser tree, watching us fix breakfast. It soon disappeared up the trunk to get its own, and a moment later we were being bombarded by pinecones. The first one just missed the oatmeal. Several more whizzed past me in rapid succession. Finally one landed in the food bag, and the squirrel ran chattering down the limb. Rangers had warned us about bears, but from here on out we were keeping our eyes open for squirrels.

Fog settled in soon after we had shouldered our backpacks. From somewhere on the unseen water came the call of a herring gull, like the cry of a sailor lost at sea. It brought to mind a tragedy that had unfolded on this coast in the fall of 1856. Heavy seas tore the rudder from the side-wheel steamer *Superior* and sent her crashing onto the rocks. Some survivors reached shelter under an overhanging ledge and watched helplessly as cold breakers washed over those still clinging to the wreckage. More than 30 lives were lost.

After a couple of miles the trail descended to Twelvemile Beach, where the escarpment turns inland. Sun began to burn through the fog. We followed a sandy bluff and then cut down to the strand, walking in time to the lift and heave of the waves. Late in the day we camped near Au Sable Point.

That night we watched the lights of a ship passing far out on the horizon. Lakemen know this treacherous shore as the Graveyard Coast and give it a wide berth. But our weather had been mild, deceptively mild.

Next morning we hiked past the iron-bolted wreckage of two wooden ships washed up on shore long since. Soon the trail reached the Au Sable lighthouse, built in 1874, and climbed steadily up the sandy flank of the Grand Sable Banks. Winds have reworked the top of the banks into an extensive field of perched dunes, anchored by tufts of marram grass. As we skirted the dunes and the pockets of jack pine sheltered between them, the weather took a sudden turn. Scott pulled on long pants over his shorts, and dug out his foul-weather gear. The temperature plunged, rain blew in from the northwest, and we plugged on to Grand Marais.

Here Scott must leave me, and I stand on the point wondering if I should go on or not. I turn away from the bitter wind and return to the village. On the way I pass an old woman walking briskly, obviously enjoying the wild weather. My doubts disappear. I'll continue alone.

To fortify myself against the cold, I stop at the Sea Gull Cafe and order a seasoned meat pie called a pasty. "My grandfather was a lumberjack and he carried them to work," the waitress tells me. "They stayed warm until lunch, and are a meal in themselves." The one she brings me could last two meals.

I pick up the trail again, thinking of going as far as the Two Hearted River. But the storm is blowing full force when I reach the shore. The entire forest bends inland, and far out on the lake waves rise in green ridges that almost take flight before collapsing in broken water. The trail runs along the higher storm beach, partially sheltered by a band of trees, but so much windfall blocks the way that I drop to the lower beach. I lean into the wind to keep from being blown over. All about me the elements have dissolved and recombined. Snow, sleet, and rain mix with wind-driven sand. Waves churn the lake bottom, turning the inshore waters sandy gray. I pass between a wall of stacked waves on one side and a wall of wind-bent trees on the other.

Blowing sand collects in every fold and pocket of my parka. Sand tendrils form behind each pebble on the beach. I walk backward for a while to let the wind work another side. This just spreads the chill, so I retreat to the trail. Trees and limbs of all sizes have fallen. Picking my way through a maze of wind-thrown debris, I try to keep on the route blazed with blue dots. Then without warning the trail leads straight off a bluff, simply disappearing into the roaring air. The storm has taken a great bite from the shore. Crashing waves are undercutting the bluff. Breakers pound against trees that have toppled into the surf. Entire stands are slumping, moss still clinging to their roots. A white birch blazed with the blue dots hangs suspended over the edge.

I detour inland, working around a tangle of windfall, listening to the skirl of wind high in the trees against the drone of windblown waves below. The going is too slow, too tiring, so I push back to the beach.

Ahead a Canada goose stands weather-stunned on a hummock of grass-anchored sand. It watches me approach, waiting until the last moment before facing the gale and spreading its wings. The wind lifts it straight into the air as it tilts south and disappears inland.

Taking the hint, I decide to head south tomorrow. I make camp not far from the Blind Sucker River, pitching my tent next to a great windfelled hemlock. Its branches may provide a buffer if another tree comes down in the night. Sitting inside, I unfold the map of the North Country Trail and trace its course. It drops downstate through lower Michigan and works deep into southern Ohio. That's where I'll go next.

By dark the winds have eased, and late at night all I hear is the hiss of light waves sweeping up the strand. The storm has passed.

The North Country Trail: Ohio

OHIO

*O*ne of the first walkers I had seen on the North Country Trail passed me at a good clip in the mist. It was a small white terrier wearing a blue raincoat. Legs moved in a blur as it tried to keep up with its master, a veteran hiker wearing a hat weighted with volksmarch emblems. A volksmarch isn't a race but an organized walk, open to all; everyone who registers and finishes the event is a winner. Still, without thinking I picked up my own pace as other volksmarchers surged past. Carried away by the general enthusiasm, I was sharing a sociable walk just after completing a solitary one.

Three days earlier, about 35 miles downstream on the Little Miami River, I had rejoined the trail as it swung through the soft farmlands of southern Ohio. I wanted to look for remnants of the region's deep-rooted history, and found some of the oldest at Fort Ancient, a hilltop site just east of the river. Here, two thousand years ago, Indians of the Hopewell culture had enclosed a hundred acres within earth and stone walls, possibly for defense, possibly for ceremonial purposes.

Aggregate crunched underfoot as I left the quiet mounds, heading north along the route of an abandoned railroad. Trains from Cincinnati to central Ohio once passed through the nearby village of Morrow—a name that caused some confusion in its time. "To go from here to Morrow and return is quite a way," ran a popular 1890s song. "You should have gone to Morrow yesterday and back today. / For if you started yesterday to Morrow, don't you see, / You could have got to Morrow and returned today at 3." But the last train to Morrow left years ago. In the early 1980s, work crews removed the tracks and ties and replaced the iron trestles with wooden footbridges. Only portions of the route have been paved as a hiking and cycling trail, but eventually a hard-surface path will run 72 miles from the outskirts of Cincinnati to Springfield—a good example of rails-to-trails conversion.

Noon under a hazy sun found me leaning against the trunk of an ancient sycamore tree, angled far out over the river. Generations of barefoot children had worn the bark smooth; a knotted rope hung from a high limb next to shredded remnants of earlier swings, ideal for splashdowns in the stream. The local squirrels seemed warier than the Upper Peninsula breed; I watched one work its way cautiously to the riverbank for a sip. Overlapping canopies of oak and maple wrapped the place in shades of green. It was a landscape made for daydreaming—unless you were a farmer who had to make a living from it.

Soon the trail took me past an old-timer driving a John Deere tractor half as old as himself. Nearby, next to a farmhouse, two men were bucking firewood; one cut as the other split. Their dog gave me a halfhearted woof before settling back to sleep on the porch.

Placid as it seems, this countryside has had its share of turbulence. For decades after the 1760s—during and after the American Revolution—Indian warriors and white newcomers fought a small-scale but bitter contest for control of it. It was a setting for desperate ventures when slavery prevailed in Kentucky, less than 50 miles away. I came upon the scene of one where Caesar Creek entered the Little Miami from the east.

Near the creek, one day in 1850 or thereabouts, a group of Quakers had gathered at their one-room meeting house. As they sat in meditation, a black man suddenly burst through the door, obviously fleeing a slave hunter. The stark room offered no concealment, but two women of goodly size spread their full skirts over the benches and told the runaway to crawl underneath. When the slave catcher entered, he saw families in silent worship. No one lied to him—no one spoke a word. A glance around the room convinced him there was nowhere a fugitive could be hiding. He departed empty-handed, wondering how the slave could have vanished.

*T*he old riverside roadbed I was following gave me a gentle grade through a rough fringe of woodland. I made good time to Waynesville, laid out in 1796, named for frontier hero "Mad Anthony" Wayne, and settled by Quakers. Strolling through the old town, I saw so many antique shops I wondered if anyone actually lived here. Then at the new library I found community historian Dennis E. Dalton, who told me something of the place.

"Anti-slavery," said Denny, "is part of the cultural essence of this town." Waynesville, he said, served as a station on the Underground Railroad, the network of routes and safe houses that funneled escaping slaves to freedom. A number of local buildings once had hidden rooms and secret stairways connected to the river by tunnels. Denny remembered from boyhood seeing the depression that marked a collapsed tunnel in the yard of a safe house.

I mentioned that I was planning to stay at inns in these historic towns, and Denny added a comment on my local choice, the Hammel House Inn. This was rebuilt with brick in 1822 to replace a log structure dating from 1799. And, he told me, it had a ghost. One night in the late 1970s a girl came face to face with an elderly stranger wearing funny-looking square-toed shoes and an old-fashioned suit with knee breeches. "She shrieked—and then watched him dissolve through the wall."

That night I settled into a four-poster for a sleep untroubled by ghosts. I saw no specters in waking hours either. By the time I was on the trail, late-morning sun had burned away the river mist to disclose a broad valley supporting prosperous farms. These well-tended farmsteads have been here long enough to have made their peace with their surroundings. One field still stood in corn, the stalks dry and brittle. As I walked past, a flock of crows exploded into the air as in Vincent van Gogh's celebrated painting—black birds against a blue sky above a yellow field.

Soon the pathway cut back to the river, where a man sat meditatively in a lawn chair placed in the middle of the stream. He had a fishing line out, but apparently just to seem practical.

Trail maintenance ended at a spot called Roxanna, but the route was passable into Spring Valley. Quakers had built the first settlement across the river and named it Transylvania, only to move it with the coming of the railroad. After spending the night at the 3 B's Bed & Breakfast, I left at first light, needing to cover more than 20 miles to Yellow Springs. Old railroad ties still lay in place along a path tangled with spiderwebs and wrapped in fog. Something moved on the path straight ahead: an apparition. Pointed ears stood up from a black shape like a Transylvanian wolf. I stopped. The creature trotted off into the woods—just a big dog after all.

From Spring Valley the trail headed straight for Xenia. Entering the city was like passing through the growth rings of a tree: the outer highway, a strip of new warehouses, a greenbelt, then the old industrial fringe, then an aging residential section. Buildings grew progressively older as the courthouse tower guided me to the center of town. On Main Street, historic buildings lined one side, modern structures the other. At a cafe I learned why. One April afternoon in 1974 a tornado tore a swath half a mile wide through the center of town, killing 34 and leaving thousands homeless.

North of Xenia, I walked a mile along a highway shoulder to Oldtown, once an important Shawnee village. I came to the field where frontiersman Simon Kenton had done some famous running. In 1778, warriors had captured him after he stole several horses. They brought him here to undergo a traditional ordeal. Children with sticks joined adults holding thorn branches and poles and clubs; they stood in two lines to form a lane six feet wide and a quarter of a mile long. At the far end was the council house. A captive would be beaten as he sprinted along the lane, but if he made it inside he was safe from whipping.

Stripped naked, Kenton started his dash, dodging blow after blow. Near the house, he knocked down one warrior but was caught and beaten groggy by others. Forced to try again, he was clubbed down by a woman and bludgeoned until he was unconscious. The leaders, who knew he had killed many warriors, decided to burn him at the stake in a village farther north. Months later, after many ordeals, he fell into British hands. He survived to tell of his exploits and died at the age of 81, a hero of pioneer Ohio.

From Oldtown I worked my way back to the railroad bed. At one point the trail was so overgrown that I detoured back to the road. Near Yellow Springs, the pathway became well maintained as it skirted Glen Helen, a nature preserve owned by Antioch University. At the Glen Helen visitor center I met the volksmarchers, some out for 10 kilometers, some for 20, and some for 30—6.2, 12.4, or 18.6 miles as measured in metric units, European style.

Originating in West Germany in 1968, *Volksmärsche* rapidly became popular in Europe. American clubs gained full international membership in 1979, and a celebration walkfest took place at Glen Helen. Now hundreds of walkers had turned out for a "celebration of leaves" on October 1. Everyone who paid the registration fee would earn a two-inch medal by completing the course. Volksmarch clubs are becoming significant among American trail users, and I couldn't mistake the enthusiasm in this group.

At the visitor center I found Milt Lord, the preservationist who had played a leading role in routing the North Country Trail along the Little Miami River and gaining scenic status for the stream. I asked if he had run into any opposition to locating the trail along the river. Some of the strongest, he said, had come from purists who opposed any change on the banks. "But once the trail's in," he added, "opposition will probably vanish overnight."

Lord has fought for more than 20 years to preserve the Little Miami and the natural areas that border it. He looked out on the deep woods of Glen Helen on the eve of their autumn splendor. "If only we didn't have these damn bulldozers." He paused for a moment, and added with a smile, "If we had to gnaw these trees down, it wouldn't be too bad."

*D*evils Lake conceals northern pike from early morning anglers.
*From East Bluff the trail overlooks this popular recreation spot. A massive ice sheet
diverted an ancient river from its valley course in the Baraboo Range.
Where ice had sealed off a portion of streambed, moraines created two natural dams:
jumbles of rocks, pebbles, silt, and sand. Glacial meltwater, snow, and rain
slowly filled the enclosed basin, giving rise to Devils Lake.*

THE
ICE AGE
TRAIL

Photographed by Tom Bean

A *high point on the Ice Age Trail, Holy Hill forms a 1,335-foot dais*
for the Shrine of Mary, Help of Christians. The low peak, known as a kame, rose when glacial
debris washed down an opening in the ice and piled up like sand in an hourglass.
Dundee Mountain, now streaked by a side trail (bottom), developed in the same way. Both kames
belong to the Kettle Moraine, an area of diverse glacial features in eastern Wisconsin.
Here hikers can trace sinuous ridges called eskers (below), molded
from deposits of streams that flowed through tunnels at the glacier's base.

*Varied soils and rocky fields tell of the Ice Age's legacy to Wisconsin agriculture.
As the last ice sheet crept into the region, uneven terrain divided the leading edge
into separate lobes. Meltwater from one lobe layered a broad plain with broken-up sandstone.
Part of the outwash area near the trail yields bell peppers picked by Carrie Diedrich
for Turner's Fresh Market on Highway 54. In Sheboygan County the Pleasant View Dairy
Farm lies where two lobes squeezed deposits into hills too rocky for plowing.
Transported by the ice, the field boulders, called erratics, came from as far away as Canada.*

*L*ive thunderbolts and surreal hues created by special use of strobe bring to light
the mythical aura of Miners Castle, twin pinnacles beside Lake Superior
in Michigan. Violent squalls come up so suddenly offshore that Indians believed
storm gods dwelled in nearby caverns. The North Country Trail,
a New York-to-North Dakota route, climbs this coastline in view of waterfalls, sand
dunes, and the bizarre cliff formations of Pictured Rocks National Lakeshore.

THE
NORTH COUNTRY
TRAIL: Michigan

Photographed by Scott Goldsmith

*S*uppertime finds Stan and Cindy Olson lighting a Coleman lantern in Tahquamenon
Falls State Park. Campgrounds dot this picturesque run of the trail.
Nearby the Tahquamenon River tumbles 48 feet, Michigan's most admired waterfall.

*B*eauty in small packages delivers scenic surprises in lakeside country. On sunny days
painted turtles surface to warm themselves. Most turtles bask, but members of
the painted clan turn sunbathing into a conspicuous show, often piling atop one another on
their favorite log. Tinged stems of wintergreen, hovering above sphagnum moss (far left),
brighten a bog. In a pine forest a weathered rock (opposite) wears a collar of reindeer lichen;
gray identifies older plants, with one seedling St.-John's-wort. On close inspection
lichens and mosses reveal patterns as fine and intricately woven as antique tapestry.

*T*assels of marram grass anchor the Grand Sable Dunes by Lake Superior.
The shifting sand rises more than 80 feet above glacial banks in Pictured Rocks National
Lakeshore. On calm days, a hike clearly reveals the immensity of the perched dunes
and the inland bent of their U-shape, molded by prevailing lake winds from the northwest.
On stormy days, gusts can quickly churn the sand into a blinding swirl.

*B*ikers pedal where trains once ran, just outside the town of Loveland in southwestern Ohio. Through this history-rich area the North Country Trail traces an old railroad route for 72 miles, always near the Little Miami River and usually set well apart from highways. Like other national scenic trails, the NCT bars all motorized vehicles. Users of this prime rail-trail conversion include equestrians, cyclists, joggers, and hikers, as well as cross-country skiers in winter.

THE NORTH COUNTRY TRAIL: Ohio

Photographed by Scott Goldsmith

*T*own and country alternate beside Ohio's trails. Cyclist Ron Geyman of
nearby Maineville pedals along the bikeway at Morrow while Toby Cain tips a pass away
from Anthony Bowman. Their Tuesday afternoon pickup game utilizes the turf strip
used by equestrians on a route that serves three systems at once: the Little Miami Scenic
Park (state), the Buckeye Trail (state), and the North Country Trail (national).
On weekends, says Geyman, joggers, hikers, bikers, and riders turn out in crowds—weather
permitting. Eventually, grassy berms will serve as footpaths and separate a paved
bike lane from the riders' track in the old rail right-of-way near Yellow Springs (opposite).
There, on her mare Brandy, high school senior Becky Rufener enjoys an outing.

*W*alkway and waterway overlap occasionally. At Loveland a steel truss railroad bridge carries the trail over O'Bannon Creek; in Greene County a trestle guides the path across the Little Miami, Ohio's first official scenic river. Pavement has replaced the foxtails and weathered timbers, as work continues to close gaps in the trail's proposed 72-mile stretch between Terrace Park and Springfield. The multi-use course offers multiple benefits. Old bridges, historic links to the age of railroads, gain a reason to remain; habitats of deer, great blue heron, beaver, and other wildlife gain a corridor of protection; and people gain a linear park for recreation. "The trail and river are a perfect scenic marriage—wooded hills, high bluffs, steep drop-offs with long vistas across meandering currents," says local outdoorsman Milt Lord. "The trail gives Midwesterners a place to experience the outdoors without leaving their own backyard. Already, users on sections of the trail in these parts number more than 5,000 on a good weekend."

*L*ife drifts at an easy pace on the Little Miami. Along the river, trekkers fall in step with country ways. At Morrow, a canoe and kayak livery—with a shaggy greeter called Pip—offers diversion. About ten winding river miles upstream, divers from Dayton sharpen their skills in the relatively clear waters of mid-October, finding "some fish and junk but no valuables," while friends keep tabs on them.

DAVID HISER

*P*oised on a minor outcrop, a hiker checks cairns marking a ridgeline section
of the Colorado Trail as sunrise tints the distant Tenmile Range. Running
between Denver and Durango, the 470-mile recreational trail passes through seven
national forests and six wilderness areas, crosses five major river systems, and climbs
eight mountain ranges. Rewards for hikers in and near the Rockies range
from sweeping vistas to the water-smoothed sandstone of narrow red-rock canyons.

THE
ROCKIES

By Cynthia Russ Ramsay

126

The Colorado Trail

COLORADO

*Y*ou can encounter a snow squall any time of year in the high country of the Colorado Trail. In summer, the flakes glaze the great jagged peaks with an ephemeral frost and blanket the alpine wildflowers, bringing a celestial sparkle to the landscape when sunlight strikes the ground. Strong winds often roil the tranquil waters of the mountain lakes into slapping, foaming waves. It can get so windy, some say, that you have whitecaps in your coffee cup. On any sunny summer day, you can also expect afternoon thunderstorms.

Capricious weather is as much a part of a journey on this trail as the meadows lush with flowers and the heights roamed by bighorn sheep. You remember the dazzling sunshine and the swirling mists as well as the warbling mountain bluebirds, the radiant reds of Indian paintbrush, and the tangy scent of spruce in the timbered valleys after a rain.

For 470 miles, the trail roller-coasters through the spectacular Rocky Mountain terrain between Waterton Canyon, outside Denver, and Durango in the southwest corner of the state. It traverses five major river systems and repeatedly crosses the Continental Divide, almost entirely on National Forest lands. Hiking the whole trail takes six weeks or more. People pedaling fat-tired mountain bikes have done it—with some detours—in less than three.

Like most people, I tackled short segments of the route, walking or riding horseback for a day or two. I began with a 15-mile day-hike, starting just west of the Copper Mountain Resort. Leading the way up from the trailhead at 9,760 feet was Randy Jacobs, a soft-spoken outdoorsman in his 30s. Since 1985, he has spent countless hours with the volunteer crews that have built 150 miles of new tread.

"Although the trail was created largely from old paths tramped by Indians, loggers, miners, and sheep ranchers, there were a number of gaps. It took many hundreds of volunteers to connect the existing pieces into one corridor. The last link-up was completed in September 1987," said Randy, slowing his pace to match mine. "Now we're working to improve the trail, and we've started building additional spur trails and access routes."

Clouds were careening out of the west as we followed a path beside a creek. Often, where willows screened it, only the melody of cascading water announced its presence. I was admiring the profusion of golden asters, harebells, daisies, and lupines that rimmed our narrow path with rich mosaics of purple and yellow blossoms. Before long, a stratus cloud, the color of steel,

*H*iking up to a maintenance party, Gudy Gaskill ruffles the fur of her
*Belgian shepherd, Shadow. President of the Colorado Trail Foundation, she campaigned
tenaciously for 17 years to make the trail a reality.*

spread a sullen darkness, bringing a cold, dank bite to the wind. We had climbed to 11,200 feet, just below timberline, where a few stunted spruce made their last stand. We wriggled into rain gear as the first drops came.

By the time we arrived at Searle Pass at 12,040 feet, the rain had turned to snow. Small, grainy flakes fell in a misty curtain that muted the tundra landscape and blurred the high peaks. But catching my breath was becoming my primary concern. We were more than two miles above sea level and I had not adjusted to the height, for at that elevation the air contains about half as much oxygen as at sea level. I broached the subject of a rest stop, and we hunkered down in the lee of some dwarf willows. "Up here, these thickets are the only way to get out of the wind because it just curls around the rocks," said Randy, sharing some oat bran wafers he had baked. I consulted *The Colorado Trail Guidebook,* which he had written, to check the elevation profile for our route: practically all downhill the rest of the way.

A series of chirps from a rocky ledge was startling in the silence. Randy spotted the yellow-bellied marmot, a rotund, furry creature the size of a fat house cat. For a few minutes it appraised us with its front paws folded across its belly. Then it shuffled away, disappearing down a crevice with a flick of its bushy tail. On these heights, almost every stone surface was encrusted with a tapestry of orange, chartreuse, and black lichens. Those mottled patterns were millennia in the making, for these complex rootless plants grow as slowly as a millimeter a year.

Resuming our hike to Kokomo Pass, we crossed level terrain with posts and stone cairns marking the route. Compact clumps of grass made it tricky going. At each step, I either wobbled on top of a tussock or sideslipped between. Intent on my footing, I didn't notice the sheep until I heard them. Ewes and lambs were calling each other in a steady chorus like a murmured chant.

Tending the flock of 1,200 was Sam Robinson, heir to five generations of sheep ranching, with his border collie, also born to the business. Sam's family has had a Forest Service grazing permit on this allotment for decades. "I'm up here from the 25th of June till the hard snows run me down about the middle of September," said Sam. "Someone has to get up real early in the morning to give sheep a direction; otherwise they scatter in all directions. It's like you threw a stick of dynamite among them."

As we talked, a wedge of blue sky appeared on the western horizon and presto, sharp-toothed peaks came into view. From our perch on Elk Ridge we could also see the remains of Bartlett Mountain, which had been whittled away by the Climax Molybdenum mine.

"We deliberately routed the trail through man-made destruction, natural devastation as from forest fires, revegetated areas, and pristine areas to make this a truly educational and scenic trail," says Gudrun Gaskill. She's the lanky, dynamic grandmother who for 17 years doggedly spearheaded the campaign to complete the trail.

Gudy's proud that colleges use the trail for outdoor classrooms in summer; that the Colorado Trail Foundation pays for two- to five-week hikes focused on history, botany, and geology; that trained crew leaders have woven lessons of ecology into the work of hundreds of volunteer trail crews. "This is one of the few trails in the United States funded and constructed almost entirely by volunteers. Thousands of people spent their weekends and vacations digging into hillsides, shoveling dirt, and prying out rocks. It was a labor of love. But without the cooperation of the Forest Service, we never could have finished the job," Gudy told me, striding along briskly.

We were walking single file up Jefferson Creek, stopping whenever Gudy spotted mushrooms. Shadow, her Belgian shepherd, romped alongside. "My dog always goes with me. So when I see a gorgeous sunset, I can talk to him and feel I've shared the moment." She stooped to pick a puffball nearly hidden by leaves. It was an old one, and when she squeezed it, spores exploded in a powdery spray. "I never keep a mushroom unless I'm absolutely sure it's edible." She noticed the warty *Boletus*, clumps of yellow coral mushroom, and the spotted *Hydnum* as she strode along.

But it wasn't a quest for mushrooms that took Gudy along this wooded path, for she wanted to check a stretch of trail that had been rerouted from a jeep road. We came to that section as we broke out of the forest into a broad basin. From a distance, patches of dainty harebells looked like lavender smudges on ground cover that already hinted of autumn. Although it was only the third week of August, an early frost had brushed the alpine avens with red.

We had almost reached the watershed of the continent, the Great Divide, when Gudy took a path that veered northeast, back to our starting point. This was one of numerous loop trails that let people take a day-hike without backtracking or arranging a car shuttle. "Someday," said Gudy, "we'll have a thousand miles of interconnecting trails that will give people unique access to some of the most beautiful terrain in the country."

*G*len Roberts gets as much pleasure being on the Colorado Trail as Gudy, but he prefers to leave the walking to horses or to Strawberry, his clever, surefooted mule. "There's nothing better than a good mule, and nothing worse than a bad one," he told me, slapping his sweat-stained fedora on his jeans. "Strawberry remembers every place we've ever been, and she can find her way through an area littered with blowdowns—fallen trees—better than any horse I know."

Glen's business, he says, is selling adventure: guiding horseback riders, fishermen, and hunters. For him, our trip through the spruce-fir forest along Silver Creek was a scouting expedition for Rocky Mountain bighorn sheep, locating the widely scattered bands before the hunting season opened in early September. For me, it was a relaxed outing, blessed with bright sunshine. We were riding along a segment of trail that threads the Collegiate Peaks Wilderness, a preserve with eight summits over 14,000 feet. No other place in the country boasts such a concentration of such high mountains.

Glen told me about bighorns. In winter, when grasses and sedges are scarce, he sets out alfalfa and apple pulp for them. He mixes the feed with medication against lungworm, one of the diseases that take a heavy toll of the scattered herds. He also takes part in a statewide program to improve the winter rangelands for Colorado's 4,000 bighorns surviving in pockets of wilderness. Though he has been leading his clients to the sheep for 18 years, he has never killed one himself. "And I hope when the sun sets on my endeavors, it can be said I put more sheep on the mountain than I took off. I try to make sure the hunters take only the very biggest, oldest ram, with horns that have grown into a full curl. By then he's ten years old and not a prime breeding animal. It's the eight-year-old that's king of the mountain." Glen stopped to study the northeast ridge of 14,196-foot Mount Yale, scanning it with binoculars.

"There're a lot of sheep there—18, but only ewes and lambs. The rams stay completely apart except for the fall rutting season." He handed me his binoculars and pointed to one area above timberline. I saw only clusters of rocks. "Look for white long johns—the white on the back of the legs—and dark faces." Glen set up a 25-power spotting scope that gave us almost a closeup view.

From a meadow in the remote La Garita Wilderness, about a hundred miles to the southwest, I was enthralled watching a herd of more than 70 elk walk in a stately procession across a grassy hillside. Two smaller animals, lighter in color, bounded after them.

"The nimble way those two are moving indicates they're deer. Elk stand as tall as a horse and move like tanks or fullbacks," said Roger Morris. He's managing editor of the *Gunnison Country Times*, a strapping, tall man, and he gave me a walking lesson as I was slogging and puffing my way up 14,014-foot San Luis Peak. This is a rounded hunk of mountain that abuts the trail and just qualifies as one of Colorado's 54 mighty "fourteeners."

"Use the mountain step," Roger advised. "Take a breath with each step, and lock the back leg as you move forward. If you walk keeping your knees bent, you're using muscle all the time. If you straighten your leg, the bones are supporting you. Over the course of a day, taking the strain off the muscles for seconds at a time makes a difference."

We had been walking for more than an hour. A ridge of crumbling rock led to the summit, a long mile away. But the alpine forget-me-nots took strain off my mind. These diminutive flowers are flecks of a blue so intense you forget everything else when you contemplate it. In the center of each blossom, smaller than a thumbtack, is a tiny ring of yellow around a red dot. It's enchanting to see something so delicate sprouting from terrain so rough.

At every rest stop Roger regaled our group with tips from his survival training classes. For example: "Black ants dropped into hot water release formic acid, which has a lemon flavor. It makes a tasty beverage, if you don't mind straining the ants through your teeth."

Well before noon we were signing the register on the summit. My pride in the accomplishment very nearly matched the pleasure of the view. Against the cobalt western sky rose the massive pyramid profiles of the San Juans, with the serrated ridges of the Needles, the spires of the Grenadiers—a vista to make one stop and consider man's place on this planet.

So was the Milky Way, seen from a mountain meadow after the peaks tapered away into darkness and the colors drained from the sky to reveal a radiant sheet of light spanning the heavens. There were other joys as well: the velvety gaze of a deer, the golden sheen of lakes in the setting sun, the sweetness of wild strawberries, the plaintive, high-pitched bugling of the elk.

And a campfire, not far from where the Rio Grande begins its journey to the sea. Gathered around were the members of a trail crew, enjoying hand-cranked wilderness ice cream made with cocoa, frozen strawberries, and canned evaporated milk, churned in a bucket filled with lingering mountain snow. I asked one of the group why he gave up his vacation to swing an ax and a grubbing tool.

"We all want to leave a mark, and this beats carving your initials in a tree," explained Bob Cutter, a lawyer and beekeeper. "This trail will last longer than any of us. It's our gift to the future."

The 10th Mountain Trail

COLORADO

*E*verything that happened while I was skiing from hut to hut on the 10th Mountain Trail grips my memory: sunset tints on summits that seem to float like clouds, the raucous cry of the raven piercing the snowy stillness, the moments of reflection by a crackling fire. Even now I can feel the rush of fear as my skis picked up speed on a steep, narrow trail.

There's more to ski touring through the high country of the Colorado Rockies than a wilderness adventure. The mountains—hard, sharp, and radiant—have a serenity that touches the soul. For accomplished skiers, who revel in swooping downhill through fluffy powder, the endless slopes of untracked snow bring a special joy. For all, there's the camaraderie that comes from sharing the challenges of winter travel in rugged terrain.

"Plodding for hours through a blizzard, taking turns breaking trail in deep snow—it really knits a group together," said Fredric "Fritz" Benedict, an Aspen architect who got his start on skis more than 70 years ago. "Meeting your basic needs—stoking the fire in the cookstove, hauling in snow to melt, keeping dry and warm and fed—creates a comfortable tranquillity. You shed the trivia that crowds the agenda of everyday life." We snapped on our skis, hoisted our backpacks, and set off for the McNamara Hut, climbing through lodgepole pines and aspens. It was a privilege to go out with Fritz, who had dreamed for years of establishing a ski route between the resort towns of Aspen and Vail. "I wanted to make it possible for more people to experience the winter wilderness, not just the hardy mountaineers who can put up with the rigors of snow camping," he explained.

In 1980, when the timing seemed right, Fritz rallied local support, started raising money, and with a small group of volunteers and the U.S. Forest Service began laying out the route. Most of the trail lies well above 9,000 feet, where snow comes early and lingers late. Wherever possible it follows old mining and logging roads, and avoids avalanche zones. The result is a 300-mile corridor that winds around snow bowls and ridges, cuts across high valleys and conifer forests, and takes the skier into landscapes of awesome beauty.

Fritz dedicated the trail to the men of the 10th Mountain Division of the U.S. Army, who trained at nearby Camp Hale, home of the famous high-country, cold-weather troops of World War II. In 1945 the division fought in northern Italy, capturing German strongholds in the Apennine Mountains.

"Basically, we were a mountain infantry without support vehicles, so we carried everything on our backs." Fritz had been a lieutenant in the 10th. "We went out with big, heavy backpacks and stiff wooden skis. At night we tunneled into the snow and simply threw branches over the entrance, but I was younger and in better shape, so it all balances out. Now 30 pounds feels like 80, and I even leave my razor home to hold down the weight."

Today skis are especially designed for touring. They're somewhat shorter and wider than regular cross-country slats, and have metal edges. They use flexible bindings that allow the heel to lift for easier climbing. It's the downhill that's difficult for skiers new to the backcountry, and the key is the telemark turn, a tricky but graceful, semi-kneeling maneuver.

Although our route was a steady uphill slog, gaining 2,000 vertical feet in six miles, I shuffled along without the backsliding that saps energy and enthusiasm. Our control came from the "skins" we affixed to the bottom of our skis. A godsend, these imitation sealskins have long hairs that dig into the snow, providing excellent traction on the upgrade.

Sheltered from the wind in a stand of timber, we took a break for lunch. To my delight, I found that eating is serious business on these trips. The huts' logbooks are brimming with details of gourmet meals—desserts like cheese-cake in a chocolate crust crowned with blueberries—lugged up in packs or cargo sleds called pulks. Exercise and the exhilarating cold create gargantuan appetites, and the bliss of it all is that you're burning so many calories, you can eat as much as you want with impunity.

By midafternoon, we reached the two-story cabin set at 10,360 feet. It was a comfortable chalet, not the shack I expected. Picture windows, solar-powered lights, and foam mattresses put these shelters in the luxury category, and the trip to the outhouse is an opportunity to admire the stars. Arrivals always set off a flurry of activity—starting a fire, dragging in big plastic garbage bags of snow and scooping it into five-gallon pots on the stoves. There's an inch of water in a foot of Colorado powder, so it takes a lot of snow just to have enough to drink, cook, and wash dishes.

Dehydration is one of the dangers of the trail. In one day of ski touring, you can lose more than a gallon of water from sweating, exhaling moist air, and the diuretic effect of the cold.

"I can't stress enough the importance of drinking lots of water to prevent headaches, nausea, or insomnia—the symptoms of altitude sickness," said Don Shefchik, expedition leader for a six-day, 35-mile trip. A wiry athlete of 40 years, Don's one of the professionals who conduct hut trips arranged by Paragon Guides. "Besides a water bottle," he went on, "a shovel is the most important thing you can carry. You always have to be prepared to dig in to create a shelter in case of an accident or a sudden serious storm."

It was evening at the Fowler/Hilliard Hut, the second stop on a trek through the White River National Forest. In the southwest, the sun cast a golden glow on Mount Elbert, at 14,433 feet the highest peak in the Rockies. Grand vistas provided the perfect end to a glistening day. Even the air had sparkled with ice crystals as atmospheric moisture condensed in the cold.

Though it had been about 10°F, I wore only a turtleneck shirt, tights, a windshell, and leg gaiters. I was comfortable as long as I was moving. Whenever we stopped, I put on a sweater, hat, and windpants. There's nothing like sweat freezing on the skin to teach you to peel off or add layers of clothing.

Not everyone spends an easy day on the trail. In one logbook I read about skiers breaking trail through deep snow in a stormy darkness: "Even our leader Big Ed showed signs of dismay as we turned another bend with still no sight of the cabin. . . . bivouacking was a real possibility."

Don leaves little to chance, for on these remote trails even a broken ski pole can spell catastrophe. His 60-pound pack holds spare gear, ski repair equipment, a sleeping bag, camp stove, a tarp for a bivouac, and a first aid kit.

But he sees his job as something more than getting people safely from one hut to another. "I'm concerned we're losing wilderness—not only the acreage but the very concept of what it means to live in tune with nature, to feel its pulse and its harmonies. Unless we discover the meaning and value of wildness, we'll not be able to preserve what remains of the wilderness," he told us.

By the fourth evening our group of strangers enjoyed an easy intimacy. Gene Tate, a taciturn man of 67, revealed that cardiac surgery had slowed him down. "But I trained for this trip by climbing mountains on weekends. The guides have a responsibility for me, but I also have a responsibility to them."

Susan Benoit, a tall, serene Vermonter, told us that sometimes she had to push herself to keep going on the trail, but she had gained a terrific sense of accomplishment. Her husband, Glenn, would go plunging down the surrounding slopes before breakfast, ecstatic as he shredded the untouched powder. On the trail he was always far ahead.

Guide Dan Ostrowski, a marathon runner with a wide smile and a magic touch for treating blisters, usually brought up the rear. His rest-stop commentary ranged over the flora and fauna of the high country. I learned that lodgepole pines are straight and tall when they grow in stands, but squat and gnarled when scattered on a windy hillside. I heard about the hunting habits of ermines, which hear voles and mice under the snow and dive in after them.

On the fifth morning, we awoke to a snowy, somber day. The telltale signs of animals—coyotes, snowshoe hares, squirrels, pine martins, and porcupines—the contours of the mountains, the patterns of the forests were all erased. I longed to remain by the wood stove. The hut never seemed cozier, the outdoors less inviting. Don was insisting on an earlier-than-usual start. As we strode into the snow-muffled silence, I heard only my breathing and saw only the furrows left by skiers in front of me. Then the path came to a steep, open bowl, where snow lay smooth and voluptuous. Before long, the sounds of our glee rang across the open spaces of winter as we plummeted—or tumbled—down the whipped-cream landscape.

The Paria Canyon Trail

UTAH

ARIZONA

A sweet, shimmering birdsong ripples through the narrow canyon, resonating against the towering expanses of sheer rock. With a trill of descending notes, the canyon wren concludes its serenade, leaving only the swish of the shallow river and the doleful sound of the chill wind gusting out of the darkness of the gorge.

I heard it in the serpentine Narrows at the upper end of the Paria Canyon, a 37-mile chasm in the arid lands astride the Utah–Arizona border. The morning sun brought a blue brightness to the slim band of sky visible from below. Light also touched the pinnacle and knob formations that crowned the cliffs, mellowing the bold terra-cotta colors of the rock into a luminous golden beige. Except for the blaze of these sky-high turrets, the stony landscape was still immersed in a diaphanous shade.

Most of the way through the Narrows I sloshed along in ankle-deep cold water opaque with silt. This informally named segment of the Paria River, seven miles more or less, is wedged between stony heights rising as much as 600 feet. At times the cliffs close in, squeezing the canyon floor to a channel 12 feet wide, with wall-to-wall water. This is no place to be when a flash flood follows one of the region's summer thunderstorms.

Even in wider reaches below the Narrows I walked in and out of the water, crisscrossing the river down to Lees Ferry, where the Paria is swallowed by the mighty Colorado River. Sometimes the streambed offered firm sand, but more often I sank into squishy mud or teetered on slippery cobbles. Now and then I experienced the small shock of stepping into a knee-deep hole. I learned to avoid shiny patches of mud, for they indicate quicksand. Although you don't sink past your shins in the Paria's "jelly mud," it's an ordeal to drag your foot out.

The treacherous going drew my attention away from the lovely intricacies of flood-polished sandstone. So I dawdled, stopping frequently to gaze up at walls whittled into sinuous contours, fluted with mighty columns, riddled with shadowy hollows, and embellished with overhangs. Water had transformed stone into eloquent sculpture.

As sunshine seeped into the Narrows, bathing the great slabs in light, I could see the undulating lines streaking the ruddy Navajo sandstone, which was formed from dunes almost 200 million years old. Swirled like taffy, the layers bear the imprint of winds rippling those sands in the age of dinosaurs.

*H*ere and there, plants found rootholds on narrow ledges and in crevices. On patches of land in old, dry meanders and along some banks, I saw clumps of dense rabbitbrush, willows, Indian rice grass, and spindly saltbush. In the wider reaches of the canyon, where thousands of years of flooding have built larger terraces, cottonwood trees spread their leafy branches. In this stark landscape, the scattered bits of greenery startle the eye. Never had the color seemed more vibrant, glowing with emerald intensity against the russet rock. The shrubby tamarisk was in bloom, and its plumes of tiny pink flowers swayed in the wind, adding a touch of delicacy to the scene. Some ecologists take a dim view of this alien plant, introduced by the Department of Agriculture early in this century for windbreaks and erosion control. Tamarisks grow rapidly into dense thickets, casting dense shade and siphoning off huge quantities of water at the expense of native plants.

For more than an hour I had hiked alone. My companions on this three-day trek—photographer David Hiser and a team from the Bureau of Land Management, which administers the Paria Canyon-Vermilion Cliffs Wilderness—were moving at a different pace through the turns and twists of the canyon. These hairpin curves kept the others out of sight, and rounding a bend was like entering a private sanctuary: a place to listen to the river, to marvel at the artistry of erosion, to sense the incredible antiquity of the earth.

Toward noon I caught up with Martha Hahn, an area manager for the BLM. An athlete, she is one of those enviable women who can spend a week in the wilderness and look as well-groomed as if she had just stepped out of her parlor. I asked her about the shiny dark streaks that patterned the cliffs like long banners decking castle walls.

"Those stripes are called desert varnish, which is nothing more than a stain produced when rain seeps down through the porous sandstone from the plateau above and leaches minerals out of the soil—mainly iron oxide and manganese oxide," she explained.

Seven miles from the White House Trailhead, where we had started out, our group reassembled at the entrance to Buckskin Gulch, a constricted side canyon. Downstream we found a good place for lunch: under an overhang and out of the sun, which had turned the river into a ribbon of glaring light. I was less interested in food than in shrugging off my backpack, heavy with water at eight pounds a gallon, and swallowing some of that weight. The BLM warns against drinking from the Paria, which may carry chemicals from agricultural runoff. With only three reliable springs in the canyon—at miles 12.3, 22.1, and 25.4—it's prudent to carry at least two quarts on a spring morning. Even more would be necessary in summer, when heat reaches 110°F or higher.

Last to arrive were Tom Folks, BLM's outdoor recreation planner for the region, and Rod "Skip" Schipper, Paria River ranger for the past ten years. Skip knows the canyon better than anyone else. The two of them had made slow progress because they were taking photographs and making an inventory of every river terrace along the way. "We record a terrace if there's something growing on it," Skip told me, propping his pack against the wall. Their immediate purpose was to identify campsites and then compare them with undisturbed plots; their ultimate objective, to determine visitor wear and tear on the landscape.

Martha explained that BLM has a twofold responsibility in managing the canyon: providing recreation for the public and preserving the wilderness qualities of the place. "To do that effectively we need to measure the carrying capacity of the land. It doesn't take too many footsteps funneling through this one corridor to trample the terraces built up by thousands of years of flooding. We must let people in," she added, "but we must also decide what is an acceptable level of change."

More visitors come to the Paria every year. In 1970 fewer than 300 people had ever made a recorded journey through the canyon. By 1989, there were 3,300 a year—30 percent of them walking its full length to Lees Ferry.

Long ago, the prehistoric Anasazi had also entered the canyon. Intriguing petroglyphs attest their passage. These Indians, who built the first pueblos and irrigation works of the Southwest in the centuries before A.D. 1300, incised boulders and walls with human figures surrounded by beasts—bighorn sheep, deer, zigzag serpents, and birds. Were these images linked to hunting practices? Do they illustrate important events or legends? Do they indicate a route to be followed? No one knows for sure.

I wondered what destination lured these industrious builders and farmers through this realm of rock. And when they came, did they also awaken to the squeaking and chattering of cliff swallows at dawn? They must have stopped at the spring where a wall blanketed with ferns drips cool water, and minnows called speckled dace flit around the tiny pools below. In spring the scent of the evening primrose was sweet then as now, and the tips of the prickly pears bore the same luscious purplish-red flowers. Surely, for the Anasazi as for me the Paria Canyon was a place of awe and enchantment.

*Llama-punchers lead a pack train above timberline on Indian Trail Ridge;
in the distance spreads Cumberland Basin, beside Kennebec Pass. Spanish conquistadors
called llamas "little camels of the Andes"; pre-Inca peoples of South America had
domesticated them about 3500 B.C. The animals' tolerance for high altitude,
small appetite, and surefootedness make them attractive to outfitters, and their padded
feet damage trails less than the shod hoofs of horses and mules.*

THE
COLORADO
TRAIL

Photographed by David Hiser

*T*eamwork builds a trail: Ignoring an August drizzle, volunteers manhandle a boulder
out of the new track that will take hikers off a jeep road. For a week of eight-hour work days,
they pay a registration fee and bring camping gear. The U.S. Forest Service
supplies a liaison official, hard hats, and tools ranging from light bowsaws to heavy axes.
The trail foundation provides an experienced crew leader, food, and gratitude.

*Flutter of crimson and golden aspen leaves heralds the onset of autumn
near San Luis Peak; the contrasting green of Engelmann spruce punctuates a snow-
dusted slope. Farther along the trail—and a couple of thousand feet higher—hikers
trudge through a light September snowstorm toward the welcome sight of
a cairn-mounted Colorado Trail marker. As the route crosses and recrosses the
Continental Divide, some high portions of the trail may remain snowbound until July,
and freezing storms can threaten the unprepared any month of the year.*

*H*eadlamps of skiers, caught by a time exposure, trace a beeline toward
Harry Gates Hut. The 10th Mountain Trail honors World War II soldiers who trained
nearby; the shelter bears the name of a veteran who survived the war.

FOLLOWING PAGES: *Mountain skier executes a kick turn across an overhanging cornice;
bright winter sunlight throws his shadow onto the explosion of snow.*

THE
10TH MOUNTAIN
TRAIL

Photographed by David Hiser

*S*now-mantled Fools Peak dominates the northern horizon beyond
Harry Gates Hut. Across the Sawatch Range to the east, Army engineers in 1942
carved Camp Hale out of the wilderness, building a training station for men of the
10th Mountain Division. Within a year 15,000 soldiers, 5,000 mules,
and a 2,000-dog K-9 unit practiced maneuvers nearby. The Rockies in winter so
impressed some of the troops they vowed to return. Fritz Benedict (above) settled
in Aspen and worked with other veterans to honor their wartime unit by establishing
a system of trails and huts between Aspen and Vail. Designed primarily for
experienced backcountry travelers, some shelters sit close enough to roads to enable
children on sleds to accompany their parents on an overnight outing.

*W*aning sunlight of a February afternoon sets aspen trunks aglow as cross-country skiers round a bend in the trail. Although blue diamonds mark major routes, snowstorms can obscure them, and users of the 10th Mountain Trail should carry a good map, compass, and altimeter, and know route-finding and first aid.

*P*ocked face of the red-rock wall reveals the weathering and erosion that cut
Paria Canyon, on the Arizona-Utah border. Hikers carry staffs for gauging stream depth
or probing for quicksand along the Paria River's banks, and in the shallows.

FOLLOWING PAGES: A lantern lights a campsite below Buckskin Gulch;
to avoid unsightly fire rings, the Bureau of Land Management prohibits campfires.

THE
PARIA CANYON
TRAIL

Photographed by David Hiser

*F*ramed by The Hole, a recess in the Navajo sandstone formation near Wrather Canyon,
officials of the Bureau of Land Management examine a pool for tadpoles and
other life. Water, which cut the canyon in the first place, remains a continuous concern
for hikers here. Big Spring, one of the three reliable sources (above), tumbles into a Sierra
cup. Each person needs to drink at least two quarts, or four pounds, a day; river water
requires purification because of contamination by livestock and agricultural chemicals in
the watershed. Finally, runoff from storms, choked between 600-foot-high
walls that may stand less than 12 feet apart, can cause flash floods at any time of year.

*R*ising moon casts no reflection on the Paria River, lost in the blackening shadows
some 800 feet below this section of the lower canyon rim. The cliffs display
the famous Navajo sandstone, as thick as 1,800 feet and formed from wind-prodded
dunes almost 200 million years old. Pale vertical streaks like those below appear
when muddy water runs down the canyon wall; shiny dark patterns of oxidized minerals,
called desert varnish, record the slow seepage of water through layers of
porous sandstone. Rock art found throughout the canyon, pecked into the weathered
stone, provides evidence of ancient human presence. The small backpackers in the scene
below may be early Hopi; the two larger figures are enigmas now.
In interpreting such figures, anthropologists mine a rich vein of speculation.

*W*esterly cloudbank shutters 10,047-foot Middle Sister, runt
of the Three Sisters Wilderness namesakes. Shunting prodigious Pacific moisture
to windward slopes, Oregon's Cascades define a sharp climatic
boundary stitched by the Pacific Crest Trail. Lava fields define the peaks' geologically
recent sputterings; volcanic soil roots towering fir and
hemlock along a stretch of the 2,600-mile Mexico-to-Canada footpath.

THE
FAR WEST

By Leslie Allen

The Pacific Crest Trail

OREGON

*y*our breathing is labored, and your aching ankles complain of overtime, yet you cannot escape the feeling that you are riding, not walking. To be exact, you're on the back of some large creature writhing its way toward daylight from a science fiction netherworld. Under your feet, its skin is like cracked leather—here rippling into dusty folds, there heaving in pangs that make your legs lurch in brief lapses of equilibrium.

Landscapes have many ways of fooling the eye and even the ear. Rarer are those that can bedevil your sense of motion as do the waves of lava, the blue ice rivers, the snowclad cones of fire of Oregon's Three Sisters Wilderness. Here the earth's features seem so new, so raw, so impermanent that a small act of imagination could set them into violent motion again. Welcome to the Pacific Crest National Scenic Trail: the back of the beast.

Riding ridgelines of California's Sierra Nevada and the Cascades in Oregon and Washington for 2,600 miles, the trail takes the measure of a rich, restless landscape. A few individuals have hiked it all, Mexico to Canada. Far more map out day hikes and short backpacking trips. In the miles I covered, from the Three Sisters area to the Columbia River Gorge, the PCT beribbons a trove of surprises. Within the Willamette and Mount Hood National Forests are loamy bowers, a few miles from moonscapes where astronauts trained. You might hike from early summer on Mount Hood's spongy meadows to fall's first stirrings by the Olallie lakes. Celebrating the Fourth of July on Mount Jefferson, you might empty snow from your boots.

The land itself is young: raised and gently rounded by shield volcanoes three million years ago, but given profile by towering stratovolcanoes, like the 10,000-foot Sisters, less than half a million years back. Lava spilling in overlapping layers across 65 square miles of the Three Sisters and Mount Washington wilderness areas has left a choppy black sea—and an ominous suggestion that the Oregon Cascades' dormancy is only fitful.

The record of this changing landscape resounds underfoot. Jabbing and brittle, like coral, lava clinks and crunches as you labor up the exposed wall that once roared molten out of Collier Cone and collided with Middle Sister's mighty Collier Glacier. Near jumbled Rock Mesa, on the pale Wickiup Plain to the south, footfalls raise cloudlets of pumice. By trickling Obsidian Falls, there is the illusion of walking over a shattered mirror when the sun shines. When it doesn't, the shards give up their magical glint and revert to the basic black of

*S*tairsteps of mossy black basalt turn glacial melt to Cubist daydream at *Ramona Falls in the Mount Hood Wilderness. Nearby trailheads offer day-trippers access; other waterfalls await northbound backpackers.*

obsidian, volcanic glass. One moment as gentle and glittery as a child's Advent calendar, the next, curtained off by menacing squalls, such scenery changes instantly. Still, as wilderness experiences go, this trail offers gentle ones, at elevations averaging 5,000 feet in Oregon.

"I feel like I'm in my backyard here," Madeleine Watters told me. Chatting by an icy spring in a creek-veined meadow, we were wrapped in scarves of fog. "The only thing that makes this place seem wild is a good storm." Even then, it's not too wild for civilized outings courtesy of Oregon Llamas, the pleasurable business of Madeleine and her husband, Tom Landis.

Trading backpack for pack animal makes special sense for those with wee ones in tow. For one trek, my husband, Greg Foote, joined me with our two-year-old, Ethan, in a child carrier. Ethan squealed merrily at the llamas toting our gear and provisions in high-tech panniers. The animals took a sphinx-like approach toward their small admirer. Enigmatic but energetic, they negotiated narrow, boulder-clogged inclines with grace. Fits of pique erupted into spats—literally—when one llama, ears swept back and long neck swiveling, puckered and took aim at another.

Llamas are valued for hair, hide, and meat as well as transport in their native Andes. In North America, they've become chic in the pricier pet set. "Llamas are a gimmick," shrugged Tom over chill-chasing curry and Willamette Valley pinot noir one night. "But they're also an appropriate way of bringing into the wilderness people who want to hike but who wouldn't backpack because they're inexperienced, or elderly, or have bad backs. Llamas make less of an impact on the trail than the lug sole on a hiking boot does."

Tom Landis calls the Three Sisters area a "weekend wilderness." The term fits other enclaves to the north, an easy drive from Portland. Overuse threatens a few five-star spots, but the "wilderness" part, as Tom explains it, is all the other places "that are beautiful, where you can go and be absolutely alone, never see another soul, and be six or eight miles from the road."

Heading into Labor Day weekend—prime-time: post-mosquitoes and pre-snow—and out of the Three Sisters, we smelled overheated car engines even before the trail briefly merges with the McKenzie Pass Scenic Highway. More a squiggle of blacktop than a highway, the road crests the Cascades through a blackened landscape. Here, like a lava igloo, stands the Dee Wright Observatory, named for a legendary local trailblazer. Each of the lookout's 11 windows frames a different mountain, and the site is like a low platform between two stairways of peaks. To the south, the Three Sisters are a stunning family portrait. Look northward, and eccentric profiles make for odder kin. Glaciers chiseled once-formidable Mount Washington down to its slender lava plug, a 7,794-foot spire, and cut Three-Fingered Jack—7,841 feet—to a mass of crags. Younger but decidedly more dignified, 10,497-foot Mount Jefferson inspired Lewis and Clark in 1806 to honor their patron and President. Beyond, on occasion, Mount Hood appears above the clouds, bright as a halo.

To the hiker, moving along at two or three miles an hour, the landscape beheld is forever in the process of becoming—changing mood as well as form. Mount Washington across lava and Mount Washington across wildflowers are different places. Moving closer to Three-Fingered Jack, you count lesser digits until you quit. In the small, huckleberry-rimmed lakes that surround it, Mount Jefferson is a reflection scattered into a hundred jigsaw pieces, but from the alpine plain of Jefferson Park it is a sky-filling force.

Mount Hood, like some elusive animal, was more often sensed than seen. Trees, or night, or weather often screened the 11,235-foot summit, Oregon's highest. Strangely enough, the peak exerted its greatest pull then. In full view, that glacier-swept cone was too alluring, and more than a little treacherous. Others have felt its magnetism. John Muir wrote of its "divine power." Backpackers and day hikers alike seek out Paradise Park, a luscious meadow on the Pacific Crest Trail's route around the mountain's southwestern flank.

Professional skiing brought Lisa Skube, my hiking companion, "to the only place in the U.S. where you can ski all summer," when she was barely out of her teens. The mountain's raw grandeur kept luring her back. "Mother Nature lets it rip up here without a second thought," she laughed. "There's a real glory to it, and you're right there in the middle of it."

Still skiing competitively, Lisa worked as a waitress at Timberline Lodge, the grand wood-and-stone landmark built and furnished by Depression-era craftsmen. Its parking lot, congested with arriving skiers, was the starting point for our 13-mile day hike across a realm of contrasts in the Mount Hood Wilderness Area. The whiteness of great glaciers and thumbnail-size wildflowers vied for attention. Just off the trail we walked silently in a little meadow until a wood grouse exploded into flight under my feet, with thunderous wing-flapping. The weather turned alternately bitter and mild every half hour. We, in tempo, donned and shed layers. On naked scree the trail disappeared; in cozy ravines it was a Mardi Gras route lined in blue lupines, scarlet paintbrush, purple asters, and goldenrod.

*F*rom the PCT, the most breathtaking thing about Mount Hood is what it's not. Glaciers have chewed up vast chunks of it, leaving voids like Zigzag Canyon, a thousand-foot switchback-riddled drop to the icy Zigzag River. Beyond where footprints peter out, past Paradise Park, are even wider, deeper, ruddier gashes.

What the forest is not can also be a revelation here. Pause to catch your breath on a ridgetop, and you may see clear-cut slopes that suggest a prize poodle shaved for a show. South of Mount Hood, gauzy screens of trees veil clear-cuts just a few yards from the trail. Near Timothy Lake, clear-cut logging right on the PCT has left openings with the scarred look of battlefields. Which is what they are, in the war between timber companies and conservationists for the future of Oregon's last unprotected old-growth groves in America's busiest logging forests. Where the trail dips toward the Columbia River Gorge, you step into the world's conifer capital. Below about 4,000 feet is a realm of giants that rule the forest as the volcanoes do the landscape.

Straight of line, tight of grain, supple yet strong, a mature Douglas fir is a lumberman's dream. The older, the better. But the virgin forests have almost all been logged. Timber companies want the rest of them. Fast-growing Doug-firs, they maintain, can easily be planted in efficient new tree farms, "managed forests" free of irrelevant species and the litter of decay.

Wendell Wood, of the Oregon Natural Resources Council, makes his living by disagreeing with that viewpoint. To show me why, he traded the great indoors for the lower-elevation forests along the trail, places he knew well. "People ask me about old-growth," he said as we shadowed a ridgeline. "Every age forest at every elevation has something unique, but old-growth is most beautiful because of the different ages and sizes of trees, the little natural openings and meadows and seeps and downed logs, the incredible diversity of plants and animals. A managed forest is uniform, with the trees all the same size."

I had admired the grand old Doug-firs and hemlocks that danced in the sky, trunks that could shelter a grand piano. Now I began to follow the light show on the forest floor. Sunbeams spotlighted a particular stump here, a clump of mushrooms there, a single pinecone somewhere else. Each, in turn, became sculptural, regained uniqueness. The multi-storied canopy that allows this quirky lightplay also helps to blunt driving snows. More than a feast for the eye, the ancient forest floor provides a winter repast of lichens and other forage for creatures large and small.

Among them, we heard the loud, shrill alarm—"eek! eek!"—of pikas in a rockpile and the rattling call of a kingfisher above a cobalt lake. A "wicka-wicka-wicka," followed by a syncopated drumbeat, announced a pileated woodpecker. I located its flashing crimson helmet high in a ragged snag.

"When a tree dies, its contribution continues," said Wendell. "Those standing snags are home to many birds and other species. You wouldn't find as many species in European forests, which are quieter because they're managed. And downed trees are at least as important as living ones to the health of the whole forest and its inhabitants."

Wonders, subtle or readily sensed, were at hand the day we hiked into the Columbia Wilderness near Wahtum Lake. My journey would end at the Columbia River Gorge, 13 miles and almost 4,000 vertical feet down the Eagle Creek Trail, a spectacularly beautiful detour from the PCT. It began, under mossy old hemlocks, in a wild cornucopia. Wendell had me tasting wild ginger (sharper than the grocery store variety), sweet Cicely pods (funky licorice), tender miner's-lettuce (definitely rabbit food). We bypassed the valerian (natural Valium), but paused to snack on tawny salmonberries (addictive) in sun-warmed openings fragrant with pitch.

Prodigious seed-bearers, the hemlocks carpeted the trail with tiny cones that crunched like spilled breakfast cereal. A permanent dew glossed everything: pencil-thin beargrass fronds, lilliputian dogwoods, eight-foot purple fireweed strung with spiderwebs, even—it seemed—the little garter snakes like glinting fishhooks. Then, high above the deepening gorge, the 18-inch wide trail became a shiny nightmare of slippery rock chipped out of dripping basalt cliffs. No safety net below this high wire of a trail.

Eagle *Creek*? A misnomer indeed for the little torrent that muscles through these rocks, carving miles of cliffs, pausing in spirit-cleansing pools, unleashing a string of magnificent waterfalls that slide out of nowhere to rage into grottoes a hundred feet below. About halfway up 150-foot Tunnel Falls the trail ducks behind the cascade. You think for a second that you're shooting the falls in a glass-walled barrel; emerging, you find yourself balancing again on your midair toehold.

The muffled rumble of a logger's diesel drifts into earshot. Time to stop and consider. Ahead lies Interstate 84, half an hour from Portland. That way lies civilization, for better (hot showers, hot meals) or worse. Back the other way is a silent argument that life's best things may not only be free, but also free of "civilizing" impulses. Right here, in the meantime, is one more waterfall, and there's still enough light for a last daydream in its thunder before the green curtain is drawn.

The Mount St. Helens Trails

WASHINGTON

Man and mountain were a curious mismatch. Alleyne Fitzherbert, Baron St. Helens, was the perfect diplomat: polished, gracious, circumspect. A skillful negotiator, he helped shape the terms of Britain's peace with her 13 rebellious colonies. As His Majesty's envoy to Madrid, he smoothed out sovereignty claims (in England's favor) to the Pacific Northwest. There explorer George Vancouver named a snowy, serene-looking Cascades peak for the baron in 1792.

Nevertheless, St. Helens might have smiled approvingly at the gentle scene that greeted one Sunday's dawn almost two centuries later. Never mind that the mountain, a volatile young volcano, had been threatening a major eruption for two months: May 18, 1980, began with the cloudless perfection Northwesterners dream of. Spirit Lake framed a seamless image of the 9,677-foot mountain. Rumpled campers made coffee under ancient Douglas firs.

Then, at 8:32, a small earthquake triggered the greatest landslide in recorded history: The volcano's entire north face simply slid away. The eruption's steam-fed force exceeded the energy of a six-megaton bomb. A lateral blast cloud, 570°F, hurtled along at 330 miles an hour. Fifty-seven human lives were lost, 230 square miles ravaged. When the main eruption was over, 1,314 feet of the summit and more than half a cubic mile of the mountain were gone. Blizzards of ashfall immobilized the Northwest, and the diplomat's name became a household word around the world.

Almost a decade later, the apocalyptic vision was still fresh and immediate. From northside Windy Ridge or minuscule Meta Lake, the usual destinations for visitors, it rolls relentlessly across slopes blanketed in millions of dead trees, like so many matchsticks. Immense flotillas of them cruise around Spirit Lake. Beyond, the mountain looks as though some careless cosmic footstep had simply crushed it. How many visitors before me had pondered this gray world as a stage set for world's end?

"This is 'America's volcano,'" ranger Hans Castren explains as we set out for the summit early one flawless summer morning. "Coming here is more than a personal thing—it's a pilgrimage for millions of people from the Northwest." As an ambitious trail-building program opens mile upon mile of this incredible place, more visitors arrive—about a million a year. Summer scrambles to the crater's south rim are so popular that most of the hundred daily permits are claimed long in advance.

The route up Monitor Ridge tastes distinctly of ashes and pumice and grit. This stuff, the texture of dry instant coffee and the color of wet cement, begins to coat your tongue near timberline. But somewhere in the boulder fields of old lava flows, not halfway to the top, I also taste humble pie. Four and a half miles from bivouac to rim, I recall myself snorting earlier. How could that possibly eat up five whole hours one way? By elevation gain. In six miles, you climb 4,563 feet. In almost four miles, from trail's end to the rim, you gain 3,663 feet, much of it a haphazard rock scramble.

Hans, a veteran, delivers a pep talk. "It's harder than people expect," he acknowledges. "It's an ordeal." I note his style: Arms akimbo, hands in pockets, he eases between rock crests and troughs with a surfer's fluidity. Some climbers want to do the last 1,500 feet on hands and knees. Getting up this dune of ash and pumice can be as dreamlike as it is grueling. Nightmarishly, you feel paralyzed when you try to hurry. Fear of falling—backward—wells up when you glance longingly at the ridgeline. Then, suddenly, you halt where the world crumbles and falls away at your feet. This is no dream.

Before you can catch your breath, the view knocks it out of you again. Just beyond your toes, cliffs drop a giddy 2,000 feet into the mile-wide crater, where steam curls from vents in the new lava dome. A sulfurous smell is swept up to you on crater gales, a ravens' playground. Ragged cliffs tilt like a crooked crown on the dark jumbled head of lava. A gnat of a helicopter hovers there, and you think of Alice in Wonderland as your perspective ratchets crazily. Through the north opening of the horseshoe-shaped crater, Mount Rainier—50 miles distant—looks close enough to touch. But Spirit Lake, just beyond the crater, seems without form or boundaries.

This amorphous stretch of blue has always played the mountain's alter ego. In 1980 the mountain's loss, so to speak, was the lake's gain. Monument naturalists describe the "bathtub effect": Plop an object into a tub full of water, and its level is displaced proportionately. Fill a lake with a mountaintop, and it doubles in surface. The naturalists remind you of the irascible 84-year-old resident, Harry Truman, and the lakeside lodge he refused to leave. They point to the far shore, trace a downward line, pause for effect: About 300 feet down, they say, is where he and his lodge might be found today. "The last time I went in, about the third week in April," says Chuck Tonn, "I brought Harry a couple of apple pies, and tried to get him to come out." He shakes his head slowly and stares at his toes. "I guess the pie plates are down there with him."

Now director of the visitor center, Chuck was 29 when he became the lake's resident ranger in 1969. Spirit Lake, he says, arm sweeping the shattered vista, "was an undiscovered paradise on a dead-end road. You really had to want to come here." To get to the lodge on the northeast shore, visitors called for a boat by hand-crank phone. Now they walk a mile from road to shore through a forest of bayonet trees. Harmony Trail is Chuck Tonn's Memory Lane. "This was a good place to watch elk," he says, scanning the trail for signs of their return. We reach what's left of Harmony Falls, and Chuck talks of the silver salmon that spawned there.

A breeze sets color moving in this moonscape. It ruffles purple fireweed, daisylike pearly everlasting, downy lupines, piquant huckleberry clusters—hardy pioneers that march right in after almost any disturbance.

"There's a lot more life than the last time I was here, a year ago," Chuck says. As we wind along Independence Pass Trail, hundreds of feet above Spirit Lake, he waves at a dozen ragged snags—nesting sites for as many birds. Pocket gophers have been busy digging. Here is a shipwrecked silver fir. Its great tangled rootball buzzes like distant lawnmowers—the sound of insects repopulating the blast zone. Another silver fir, only two feet high, survived the blast under the stubborn snowpack of a north-facing slope. The greening of Mount St. Helens is most evident to eyes like Chuck Tonn's, eyes with a memory. To newcomers, the future is more imaginable than the past. I fight off disbelief when Chuck says that the landslide and the lateral blast may have hurled all the lake's water out of its bed. Rumors in 1980 insisted that Spirit Lake had disappeared forever. To squelch them, the quarter-mile squiggle to the Independence Pass overlook was hacked through the blast zone in 1982. Four years and three miles later, the trail reached Norway Pass, some 1,400 feet above the present lake level. When we reach it, Chuck says in an offhand way, "The waves splashed almost up to here." Our search for a propane tank, said to have crested the cliffs on boiling waves, proves fruitless. But it scales the cataclysm down to personal range.

So do the hikes themselves. Most offer unexpected challenge of one kind or another. Independence Pass Trail, for instance, begins with a gentle uphill stroll through harmonizing purples—asters, fireweed, thistles—and ends in a similar mood. But in between, bristling pinnacles punctuate a hair-raising meander along cliffs scoured and primed for slides. The popcorn-size pumice is slippery; sunlight ricochets off the ash and glares in unshielded eyes.

Peril and pleasure rub elbows on other trails. That, according to the monument's trail planner Randy Peterson, is the whole idea for the Lava Canyon trail, still unfinished at the time of my visit. Bureaucracy works in dry terms— "perceived risk," "actual risk"—but here it acknowledges the Tarzan in us all. In 1980 the Muddy River lahar, a slurry of floodwater and volcanic debris, raced through this secluded sliver of a southside gorge and uncloaked a sculpture garden of sinuous ancient basalt. The three-mile trail built in its wake includes a barrier-free boardwalk, a harrowing stretch along the cliff face, and a 30-foot ladder up a sheer curtain of rock. Hikers must supply their own bravado. The adrenalin is free, as on other trails hereabouts. And the occasional jolt—the brief, sweat-breaking sense of danger—is appropriate, lest the quiescent volcano lull you into a sense of nature subdued.

The Santa Barbara Trails

CALIFORNIA

*J*ust off the California shore, the rigs pump a steady supply of crude from seafloor oil fields. In Santa Barbara itself another liquid has become nearly as valuable. Water still traps sunlight in the glittering emeralds of estate swimming pools and drip by drip it muddies a shady mountainside trail. But the arroyos are crusty and the cool swimming holes in the canyons a memory. It's only April: Already small brushfires erupt in the Los Padres National Forest. (In June fire will invade the city and claim at least 438 homes.) Already trailside chaparral feels feathery, crunchy, and tindery.

In 1990, the fourth year of an insidious drought, I went climbing near Santa Barbara and discovered on its steep Front Country trails the raw power of water—or lack of it—to shape life in California's southland. Backyard and barricade to the resort city of 82,500, the low-slung Santa Ynez Mountains crowd Santa Barbara onto a southerly coastal strip. At night, the city becomes an island of light hemmed by blackness—the Pacific, the 50-mile mountain wall skimming 4,000 feet, wilderness back country beyond. By day, the mountains' east-west orientation combines with the tilt of their cityside Front Country slopes to catch the sun's rays at parching, head-on angles much of the year.

During a turn-of-the-century "water famine," Tunnel Trail served excavators in Mission Canyon as they bored through four miles of mountain sandstone and shale to complete the world's longest tunnel for drinking water. A century earlier in neighboring canyons, Spanish padres and Chumash Indian workmen harnessed tumbling creeks to supply the mission.

Standing under a welcome arch of shade, I mentally rebuild a low, ragged fieldstone wall into a dam. Giving Mission Creek's slow trickle a role in the Spanish Empire is trickier. To my companion Jim Blakley, however, the dam is but a small example of the ingenuity a spare land can breed.

Retired botanist, inveterate hiker, local historian, Jim can read trails and their contexts at waterfall speed. We're near the trailhead of three-mile-long Rattlesnake Canyon Trail, on an old buggy road. Jim toes a deep rut. "Might be from the quicksilver mining days, back in the 1870s. That's when this trail got a lot of use." An old side trail, more gully than anything, takes off into the brush, and so does Jim's narrative of Indian paths trampled into cattle routes, of Spanish rancheros and Anglo homesteaders. By 1900, the new U.S. Forest Service had blazed trails through reserves set up to husband water.

*N*ow the trail narrows and climbs through elfin forest, yellow sandstone cliffs and fault-torn rock faces, sunny meadows, moist creek bed. Jim points out the key distinction—"hard" versus "soft"—in the grayish chaparral. Scrub oak lends its Spanish name, *chaparro*, to both, but belongs to the hard category. So do manzanita, mountain mahogany, and other densely packed, shrubby species that discourage cross-country bushwhacking much as barbed wire would. Jim confirms: "You'd get cut to ribbons out there."

The soft chaparral community of the lower slopes is a sensory antidote. There are velvety, minty leaves; splashy yellow monkeyflowers; purple, black, and white sages that explode with fragrance in springtime. On burnt-over meadows, soft chaparral unfurls tender young shoots like flags planted on the moon. Wildfires are the chaparral's literal life sparks. Jim names some of the bigger ones—the Coyote Fire, the Refugio Fire—and points out gnarled webs of dead brush. Thirty years into its life cycle, half the chaparral may be dead tinder. Its own resins and volatile oils, with their seductive aromas, feed flame as effectively as gasoline.

Chaparral country opens slowly to enjoyment. On the deeply worn trail that winds up Cold Springs Canyon, I discover creekside luxury amid slopes charred by the Coyote Fire in 1964. Willow, alder, bay, and sycamore thrive on the moisture, shading wild roses and other flowering shrubs. A little higher up, elegant stands of live oaks canopy the trail. Lines of rich lime-green drip like spilled paint down pale hillsides from the namesake springs. Our only companions on the trail are the little gray-green lizards that scuttle across it.

The chaparral's subdued layerings only seem disconnected from the concerns of Santa Barbara's palmy boulevards, a ten-minute drive from the trailhead. On the Hot Springs Trail, I come upon a pipe leaking warm water onto the path. Strands of algae wave languidly in milky, sulfurous little puddles. Ahead, more pipes cross the trail. Here, mighty forces vie for little Hot Springs Creek. A century-old private company pipes the water down to the lawns of nearby estates; shares, when available, sell for thousands of dollars each. In the past, hikers and hot-springs enthusiasts have siphoned untapped water into makeshift spas; company officials have tolerated the hikers but dismantled the rock-and-tarp tubs.

Thick stands of bamboo rustle along the last segment of the mile-and-a-half trail. Banana and avocado trees, palms and red geraniums ring one of them. But the crumbling foundation walls of an old resort, thrice destroyed by wildfire, are stark reminders of a larger reality.

A century ago, downstream landowners were already griping about spa-bound trespassers. Once the carriage road for the resort, Hot Springs Trail stitches the property lines of baronial spreads—mansions of movie stars, rock idols, and corporate executives—near the trailhead. Since my visit, it has been closed to hikers, with a padlocked gate. Nevertheless, Vivian Obern, a long-time trails advocate, reports that the situation may yet be resolved to admit them, by diverting the route from the springs. A patchwork of legal arrangements, and ongoing litigation, may permit or prevent access through private property on other historic Front Country trails.

Only one of these, up Romero Canyon, lies entirely within the boundaries of Los Padres National Forest. "And that's been taken over by mountain bikes," laments Vie Obern. She's a horsewoman who feels that speeding cyclists endanger horses and hikers. Bikers, of course, dispute that. "In any sport, you're going to have a few reckless individuals who get all the attention," says Bill King, active in both mountain biking and trails preservation.

Cheaper than horses, the bikes appeal to a time-pressed generation. I understood why when I panted and pedaled my way up Romero Canyon on a 21-gear, chunky-wheeled mountain marvel. Swerving around stones, bouncing through gullies, squeezing hand brakes left me no time to scan my surroundings. Still, as Linda King, Bill's wife, points out, "With mountain biking, you can get on a trail before or after work and go a long way."

Whatever the competing claims on them, the trails channel body and mind toward wilder, subtler realms. One Santa Barbaran who writes extensively on the Santa Ynez Mountains, Ray Ford, encourages off-trail exploration, "sliding slowly and obliquely through the chaparral as you would move through a crowd." The rewards, he says, are "lots of hidden places that are there to find."

Places like The Playground: several square miles of exposed bedrock that has eroded into a wonderland of huge, sunlit boulders and damp caves, of tawny arches and impossibly narrow chimneys and deep, bridgeless crevasses. A rude trail leads into The Playground from a road near San Marcos Pass, but maps ignore it. Ray's students found the spot several years earlier, and he has made a ritual of returning with new crops of highschoolers. One day I joined them. We climbed, slid, leaped, and crawled around The Playground while afternoon stretched hawks' shadows across the rocks. I felt about 14 myself. Fantasies, everyone knows, can take root in this dry green-gold land. Ray told me that teamwork and "new sets of rules" also grow among the students he brings to explore the Front Country. And the combination, I thought, came pretty close to an ideal of the high country west.

Depression-era landmark, Paradise Park's shelter offers the weary rest and hikers a rendezvous near Mount Hood's peak-girdling Timberline Trail, which joins the Pacific Crest Trail for some 18 miles. Nestled at 5,600 feet—more than a mile beneath Oregon's loftiest summit—the alpine meadow is famed, and perhaps named, for carnivals of summer wildflowers blooming close to snowpatches. Overuse has menaced it. Campers must find sites outside the meadow.

THE
PACIFIC CREST
TRAIL

Photographed by Rich Frishman

*F*lag of life planted in an earthly moonscape, a mountain hemlock survives in Belknap
Crater's lava fields, north of the Three Sisters; wind-borne nutrients help
sustain it. Perhaps a century old, it has reached the height of a ranger's waist; in more
hospitable settings this hardy conifer, ubiquitous in the Cascades, may soar to 115 feet.
Lightning or wind lopped off most of the mature specimen that lightens solo
hiker George Woodard's load—but only briefly. He completed his Mexico-to-Canada
marathon in a total of five brisk-paced months, in two consecutive summers.

*S*carlet bracts of the Indian paintbrush, a common wildflower, gladden slopes
from early summer until autumn. Nature's palette tints shady forest floors more subtly.
Patchy mottlings denote an Amanita, *the vision-inducing fly agaric*
of mycologists' lore; Russula's *fan-like gills sprout from sphagnum moss.*

FOLLOWING PAGES: *Mount Hood's glacier-gouged canyons mean unexpected*
ups-and-downs for unwary hikers, many of whom set out from
Timberline Lodge (at left). On the skyline at right rises snowcapped Mount Adams;
to the left, the distinctive flattened summit of Mount St. Helens.

*B*lowdown thatches Mount St. Helens nearly a decade after the blast—
"so many capriciously strewn matchsticks," to the author. Below Norway Pass Trail,
about five miles from the crater, Route 26 winds north to Randle, the nearest town.
Amid perspective-shattering vistas, swaths of green orient hikers: Shady north
and northeast slopes, like those at lower right, lagged behind spring thaw on May 18,
1980. Saplings then buffered by snowpack crown the landscape now.

THE
MOUNT ST. HELENS
TRAILS

Photographed by Rich Frishman

Like a broken eggshell, mountain flanks cup the 2,000-foot-deep crater and lava dome growing within it. Rim contours crumble where the 1980 landslide and eruption blew half a cubic mile of mountain, including 1,314 feet of summit, north toward Mount Rainier. At Windy Ridge, four miles away, temperatures rocketed to 570°F, and winds to 250 miles per hour. Windbreaker weather prevails there, as visitors zigzag between lookouts on a log ladder anchored by cables.

*O*therworldly vistas reward a couple who managed the grueling hike to the south rim.
Despite boulders, airborne ash, and punishing elevation gains, thousands clamor
for one-day passes up Monitor Ridge. Beyond the Pumice Plain and Spirit Lake, faintly
greening ridges hint at the landscape's past and future. So does the lava dome,
built to more than 1,000 feet by several small eruptions. Eventually, the growth of the dome
might fill in the crater and restore Mount St. Helens to a semblance of its former
serenity—as in the postcard-pretty vista seen (before and after) from Norway Pass.

*S*elf-proclaimed "Los Padres Drifter" Andy Witmer—advertising "some cow work,
talltales, free advice"—puts pack stock through its paces at Inspiration Point
on Jesusita Trail; his tenderfooted terrier, Biggy, gets a ride. Linking San Roque and
Mission Canyons, the trail crosses suburb, ranchland, creek bed, woodland,
and exposed sandstone before joining a power-line road. Sunsets suggest the overlook's
name, as the Santa Barbara Channel frames clustered city lights.

THE
SANTA BARBARA
TRAILS

Photographed by Ana M. Venegas

*O*ff-trail amusements absorb hikers along for the Sierra Club's regular Saturday outing.
Santa Barbaran Veronique La Via pauses with pet lovebird Piccolo amid scrub
oak and chaparral, evergreens just beginning spring growth spurts. Elsewhere, April carpets
meadows with wildflowers; an adult inhales their fragrance while a child plucks
an illegal nosegay. Sunshine alone can prompt blossoms of the state flower—
Eschscholzia californica, or California poppy—to unfurl. Fragile-looking creamcups,
here set off by purple brodiaea, grow profusely on burnt-over land.

*O*n foot for a change, equestrians Vivian and George Obern stroll near ridgetop-crowning bedrock minutes from metropolitan bustle. By hook, crook, committee, or lawsuit, Vie battles to keep open historic but challenged rights-of-way.

*B*aseball and biking mix in northern Virginia, where cyclists in Washington & Old
Dominion Railroad Regional Park cheer players at Arlington's Bluemont Park.
A 100-foot-wide ribbon of green created from abandoned railroad right-of-way, the W&OD
links parks, towns, and neighborhoods for 45 miles from the Potomac River to
the Blue Ridge Mountains of rural Virginia. One of the busiest converted rail-trails,
it attracts more than two million joggers, hikers, bikers, and horseback riders every year.

EPILOGUE

By Ron Fisher

*T*he trains stopped running through West Chester a few years ago, but the roadbed is still there, and one recent May I went for a walk along it. Some things have changed, I found, and some have remained the same. The cinders no longer crunch underfoot, but the orioles and chickadees are still there, and the path leads ever toward something unexpected. A dog and a groundhog, out in front of me and my companions, were so interested in us that they didn't see each other. I focused my binoculars on the groundhog, which was between us and the dog. It turned and fled toward the dog, and it looked for a moment as if there would be a head-on collision. But the groundhog detoured into the trailside grass at the last second.

My sister Kathy stopped every few feet to examine the wildflowers and grasses of the vicinity. Wild geraniums, spring beauty, bloodroot, wild ginger. "This is waterleaf," she said. "See how the leaves look like they've been stained by water, like an old piece of paper." Jacob's ladder, golden Alexanders, columbine, a wild cherry sapling in bloom. Blue-eyed grass. "It's not really a grass. Akin to iris." Prairie clover, prairie coneflower, prairie phlox, prairie willow, prairie violets. Around us, shrubs and bushes rang with the chirps and whistles of towhees and indigo buntings, cowbirds and catbirds, warblers and dickcissels and grosbeaks.

But there had been some significant changes, too. The line's metal rails and heavy wooden ties had been removed and the roadbed smoothed. My old railroad line was now officially a trail. The Kewash Nature Trail, 14.8 miles long and 100 feet wide, runs flat, straight, and smooth between Keota and Washington, Iowa. At the halfway point is West Chester.

A nonprofit organization in Washington, D.C., the Rails-to-Trails Conservancy, is helping citizen groups all over the country convert abandoned rights-of-way into trails. Every year, it reports, railroad companies abandon approximately 3,000 miles of track, and much of that roadbed is ideal for hiking, biking, and cross-country skiing. The corridors are flat or slight of gradient, and easily adapted to use by the handicapped; they're steeped in romance and history, good wildlife habitat, effective shelterbelts, and often surprisingly scenic. A mere 200 acres of right-of-way can produce a park more than 20 miles long. Many of tomorrow's trails will likely derive from yesterday's rail lines.

On my nostalgia hike with Kathy, we had a special companion: Mike Zahs, president of the Kewash Nature Trail Association. "Our little communities raised $35,000 to buy this corridor and $8,000 to renovate it," he told me. "Contributions came from between 600 and 700 people, and only one was for more than $1,000, so support was widespread."

We stopped at an old iron bridge across Crooked Creek. Volunteers had put down a concrete deck just the week before. "This bridge was built in 1871," said Mike, "and it's still so strong an engineer recently certified it 'for any load.' They don't build 'em like that anymore."

Opposition to the project came primarily from farmers who wanted the land to "revert" to them, though in fact it had not yet been cultivated when the railroad bought it in the 1870s. "If it's going to revert to anyone," someone commented, "it should be to the Indians." Other opposition was just "ornery," said Mike. "Anti for the sake of being anti."

In the future, we are likely to find more and more trails developed the same way as the little Kewash Nature Trail. There will be proposals by groups of local citizens, volunteer labor and private fund-raising, assistance from various state or national organizations and government agencies, opposition that withers in the face of education and trouble-free seasons. Trails in or near cities will become increasingly popular as the country becomes more urbanized. Reston, a planned community of 56,000 people in northern Virginia, has about 70 miles of pathways among its streets and shops.

In this respect, the trails movement continues a historical pattern. New England, with its towns and cities and early industrialization, led the way a century ago. Northeasterners have taken a leading role in other regions, from Benton MacKaye's activities in the southern mountains to Jim Kern's in Florida. As a region of rural realities and traditions, the Southeast came late to the cult of trails. "In the 1950s," remarks a native, "the political mileage was still in paving farm roads. Anybody who wanted to walk in the country could find an old dirt road with no trouble at all, but not many people walked just for the fun of it."

According to a recent study, southerners are still less given to hiking than people of other sections, but walking is by far the most popular trail activity in the nation. More women walk for pleasure than men, and more women ride horseback. Both riding and backpacking are more popular in the West than elsewhere, and so is running, which appeals strongly to blacks. Bicyclists devote the most time to their specialty, canoeists and kayakers the least—although their numbers have quadrupled since the 1960s. Obviously there is a clientele for specialized and multi-use routes.

The 1,250-mile Buckeye Trail, which completely encircles Ohio, is a good example of a multi-use trail. In urban areas, it passes through city parks where joggers and commuters enjoy it. In the countryside, hikers share it with cyclists and equestrians; its sponsors even permit the controversial mountain bikes in some locations. In winter, skiers and snowshoers take over, and history buffs can trace abandoned canal systems at any season.

Hiking inn-to-inn is a fashionable alternative to roughing it in Vermont. Twelve country hostels there, strung near a hundred-mile section of the Long Trail, offer walkers the fun of the hills without the drudgery of carrying a heavy backpack. Hikers eat and sleep at a different inn each night.

Horseback riders, motorbikers, and others in New England have successfully launched the Southern New England Trunkline Trail, which runs along abandoned roadbeds in Massachusetts and Connecticut—once the New York, New Haven, & Hartford tracks. Canoe trails in Everglades National Park offer trips of several days' duration; charts and a compass are needed for navigating the twisting and branching sloughs, creeks, lakes, and bays. The 20,000-member Vermont Association of Snow Travelers maintains 2,200 miles of groomed snowmobile trails and 2,500 miles of secondary trails—80 percent of this on private land. Across the continent, volunteers in Washington State maintain more than 500 miles of trail in the Wenatchee National Forest for off-road motorcycles and four-wheel-drive vehicles.

In spite of funding problems, bureaucratic indifference, and landowner opposition, the future of trails in this country seems fairly bright. As long as people love to feel the outdoors around them, grass or cinders or even snow beneath their feet, there will be pathways to discovery.

So go ahead. Try it. Get yourself a small daypack and a canteen, some sunscreen and insect repellent, a field guide to birds and another to wildflowers, some binoculars and a camera. Pack 'em up. Hit the trail.

*P*lowed fields cleave the Cedar Valley Nature Trail, the only break in its tree-lined
course through east-central Iowa. Created from abandoned right-of-way of the Waterloo, Cedar
Falls, and Northern Railroad and designated a national recreation trail in 1984,
the 53-mile greenway cut through cropland. Farmers opposed the trail; in 1988 Edward
McKinley bulldozed the 2,000-foot section that his farm straddles. The Supreme Court of Iowa
ruled that the land belonged to the McKinleys, but a new law allows the state to acquire
it by eminent domain. For now bicyclists Ed and Sandy Colton of Cedar Rapids—and others
like them—must detour around the McKinley furrows. Looking ahead, users can
assure the existence of future trails and the health of the national system.

Notes on Contributors

Free-lance author **Leslie Allen** was a member of the Society's staff from 1978 till 1989. Among her notable contributions is *Liberty: The Statue and the American Dream,* prepared by the Society and published by the Statue of Liberty-Ellis Island Foundation, Inc., in 1988.

Thomas B. Allen, a member of the Book Service staff from 1965 to 1981 and author of the Special Publication *Vanishing Wildlife of North America,* has continued to write for the Society as a free lance. He is also co-author of a forthcoming reference work on World War II.

Park ranger turned free-lance photographer, **Tom Bean** has been hiking trails on Society assignments since 1984. A frequent contributor to NATIONAL GEOGRAPHIC TRAVELER, he has also done chapter coverage for books, including the forthcoming *Grand Canyon Country.*

Since 1978, free-lance photographer **Annie Griffiths Belt** has worked on more than two dozen magazine and book projects for the Society. Her current assignments are the Special Publication *Heartland of a Continent* and a NATIONAL GEOGRAPHIC article on Vancouver, British Columbia.

Ron Fisher joined the Society's staff in 1962. He has written two books on hiking the Appalachian Trail as well as a large-format study of the federal lands, *Our Threatened Inheritance,* and the forthcoming *Heartland of a Continent.*

Rich Frishman, who has been taking pictures since age five, became a free lance in 1984 after several years of newspaper work. A resident of Washington State, he brings his love of the outdoors to his craft.

A photography intern at NATIONAL GEOGRAPHIC in 1979, **Raymond Gehman** is currently on the staff of the *Virginian-Pilot* and *Ledger-Star* in Norfolk. His assignments for the Society include *America's Outdoor Wonders: State Parks and Sanctuaries* and the recent *Yellowstone Country.*

After graduating from Indiana University in 1980, **Scott Goldsmith** became a staff photographer for the *Courier-Journal* in Louisville, Kentucky. He has been a free lance since 1986; this is his first Society assignment.

Since 1968, free lance **David Hiser** has photographed 20 articles for NATIONAL GEOGRAPHIC and contributed to as many books for the Society. A hiker, mountain climber, and river runner, he made the dust-jacket picture for this book a few miles from his home in Aspen, Colorado.

Robb Kendrick, a Texan now based in New York, left East Texas State in 1986 to become a photography intern with the GEOGRAPHIC. Since then his work has appeared in a variety of books and magazines.

A Society staff member from 1970 to 1990, **Jane R. McCauley** contributed to all the products of Special Publications. In 1989 she reported on "The Roads Less Traveled" for *New England.* As a contract author, she is currently writing her tenth book for young children, *Dinnertime for Animals.*

Staff veteran **Cynthia Russ Ramsay** has written for more than 20 Special Publications, traveling in the U.S. and abroad, skiing whenever possible. For the forthcoming *Beyond the Horizon,* she took a pirogue voyage down the Niger river in the West African nation of Mali.

Born in Oklahoma but reared in Nebraska, **Joel Sartore** is now the director of photography for the

SCOTT GOLDSMITH

WET FOOTGEAR DRIES AT A CAMPFIRE.

Wichita *Eagle.* As a free lance, he has been covering the plains and prairie states for *Heartland of a Continent.*

Now a free lance, **Pete Souza** worked as an official White House photographer from 1983 till 1989, documenting the Reagan years. His work has appeared in magazines around the world; this is his first Society assignment.

In more than 20 years of photography, **Medford Taylor** has carried out varied assignments for the Society, including the Special Publication *Excursion to Enchantment,* articles for TRAVELER, and recent coverage of Australia's Simpson Desert for NATIONAL GEOGRAPHIC.

Free-lance writer **Scott Thybony** described the Heard Museum in Phoenix for the winter 1987-1988 issue of TRAVELER; in 1988 he received the Lowell Thomas Award given by the Society of American Travel Writers for "best cultural tourism article" of the year.

Ana M. Venegas, another of the Society's photography interns, graduated from the University of Texas in 1987. She now lives in California, working as a staff photographer for the *Orange County Register.*

Acknowledgments

The Special Publications Division gratefully acknowledges the generous cooperation of individuals and organizations named, portrayed, or quoted in this book. For perspective and general guidance, we thank David M. Sherman, now of the U.S. Forest Service and formerly of the National Park Service, as well as Thomas L. Gilbert and Steven Elkinton of NPS. Personnel of these agencies and of the Bureau of Land Management have helped with many details, as have other federal, state, and local officials and private citizens. Officers and members of trail associations and councils have eased our way throughout the preparation of this book. In particular, we thank those cited here: Gerald D. Baumann, Raymond Bergeron, Gregg L. Bruff, Janaye Byergo, Lee Clayton, Edwin Dale, Charles E. Dressler, Elizabeth C. Dudley, Sylvia Dunnam, Don F. Fig, Jack K. Fletcher, Wilson Francis, Walter Graff, Miles Henstrom, Aline LaForge, Kenneth I. Lange, Susan Lester, Peter Looram, Edward MacKay, Charles B. Monson, Tom F. Neenan, Roger Reif, Phillip R. Shriver, Robert K. Strosnider, Charles Thiemann, Fred H. Young.

Index

Boldface indicates illustrations;
italic refers to picture captions.

Additional Reading

Readers may wish to consult the *National Geographic Index* for related articles and books; of special relevance is Ron Fisher's 1988 account of the Appalachian Trail, *Mountain Adventure.*

The following may also prove useful: The Appalachian Mountain Club, *AMC White Mountain Guide;* Arthur Benkaim, *Santa Barbara Trail Guide;* Louis W. Dawson II, *Colorado's 10th Mountain Trails;* Ray Ford, *Day Hikes of the Santa Barbara Foothills;* Jean Craighead George, *The American Walk Book;* The Green Mountain Club, *Guide Book of the Long Trail;* Randy Jacobs, *The Colorado Trail;* Michael R. Kelsey, *Hiking and Exploring the Paria River;* William E. Reifsnyder, *High Huts of the White Mountains;* Henry S. Reuss, *On the Trail of the Ice Age;* Robert H. Ruchhoft, *Kentucky's Land of the Arches;* Jeffrey P. Schaffer and Andy Selters, *The Pacific Crest Trail;* Scott Shane, *Discovering Mount St. Helens;* Laura and Guy Waterman, *Forest and Crag.*

Library of Congress CIP Data
Pathways to discovery : exploring America's national trails / prepared by the Special
Publications Division, National Geographic Society.
    p.   cm.
    Includes bibliographical references (p.   ) and index.
ISBN 0-87044-792-0
1. Trails—United States. 2. National parks and reserves—United States. 3. United
States—Description and travel—1981- I. National Geographic Society (U.S.). Special
Publications Division.   E160.P19 1991   917.3'0943—dc20   90-20750   CIP

Composition for this book by the Typographic section of National
Geographic Production Services, Pre-Press Division. Set in Palatino. Printed
and bound by R. R. Donnelley & Sons, Willard, Ohio. Color separations by
Graphic Art Service, Inc., Nashville, Tenn.; Lanman Progressive Co.,
Washington, D.C.; Lincoln Graphics, Inc., Cherry Hill, N.J.; and Empress
Graphics, Inc., Scarborough, Ont., Canada. Dust jacket printed by
Federated Lithographers-Printers, Inc., Providence, R.I.